Russia Goes to the Polls

Studies in Soviet History and Society

edited by Joseph S. Berliner, Seweryn Bialer,
and Sheila Fitzpatrick

Russia Goes to the Polls

The Election to the
All-Russian Constituent Assembly, 1917

Oliver H. Radkey

WITH A FOREWORD BY
Sheila Fitzpatrick

CORNELL UNIVERSITY PRESS

Ithaca and London

First published 1989 by Cornell University Press.

Library of Congress Cataloging-in-Publication Data

Radkey, Oliver H., 1909–
    Russia goes to the polls : the election to the all-Russian Constituent Assembly,
1917 / Oliver H. Radkey ; with a foreword by Sheila Fitzpatrick.
        p.   cm.—(Studies in Soviet history and society)
    Enl. ed. of: The election to the Russian Constituent Assembly of 1917. 1950.
    Includes bibliographical references.
    ISBN 0-8014-2360-0 (alk. paper)
    1. Vserossiĭskoe uchreditel'noe sobranie (1918 : Petrograd,
R.S.F.S.R.)   2. Elections—Soviet Union—History—20th century.
3. Soviet Union—Politics and government—1917–1936.   I. Radkey,
Oliver H., 1909–   Election to the Russian Constituent Assembly of
1917.   II. Title.   III. Series: Studies in Soviet history and
society (Ithaca, N.Y.)
    JN6594.R34   1989
    324.947'0841—dc19   89-42884

Printed in the United States of America

⊗The paper used in this publication meets the minimum requirements of the
American National Standard for Permanence of Paper for Printed Library Materials Z39.48–1984.

TO JAKOBA AND INGRID

CONTENTS

PART THREE
TABLES

FOREWORD

OLIVER RADKEY'S *Election to the Russian Constituent Assembly
of 1917*, published in 1950 and long out of print, is a classic whose
reappearance would have been very welcome even without the
new material he provides in *Russia Goes to the Polls*. The
Election, which is reprinted as Part One of this volume, is a
clear, scrupulous, and thorough analysis of the voting in Russia's
only free national election, organized under the Provisional Government but actually held shortly after the Bolsheviks' seizure of
power in Petrograd in October 1917. The Constituent Assembly
itself was a short-lived body, forcibly dissolved by the Bolsheviks
a few days after its first meeting, and of small historical significance. But the election is and will always remain an object of
keen interest to students of the Russian Revolution.

The reason is that the voting is the best barometer we have of
national popular opinion at the time the Bolsheviks took power.
Historians are always going to argue about the extent of the
Bolsheviks' popular support and the broader issue of the legiti-
macy of Bolshevik rule. But in recent years this has become a
particularly charged issue in Western scholarship, since "revisionist" historians have challenged—and to a large extent suc-
cessfully, as far as scholarly and student opinion is concerned—
the earlier assumption of most Sovietologists that the Bolsheviks
were without any real popular mandate at the time they took
power. Many students now come into classes on the Russian
Revolution accepting revisionist premises, whereas ten or fifteen
years ago, most of them had the opposite assumption.

Actually, as Radkey's book very elegantly shows, the issue of
popular support and political preference in 1917 is an enor-
mously complex one. The Bolsheviks, who won 23.7 percent of
the national vote, according to Radkey's revised calculations, but

carried the big industrial cities and large sections of the army vote, came in second to the Socialist Revolutionary (SR) party, traditionally the "peasant" party. The SRs won 37.3 percent of the national vote, mainly because of heavy peasant support. But the SR party had split, though too late for its two factions to be distinguished at the polls, and the Left SR platform was almost indistinguishable from the Bolshevik one. Moreover, as Radkey demonstrates in the discussion of peasant voting that is one of the analytical and expository tours de force of this book, peasants in areas close to cities, railroads, and garrisons—those who were most likely to know what the Bolshevik party stood for—tended to split their vote between SRs and Bolsheviks.

Radkey's *Election* has always been a godsend for teaching purposes. In the 1970s, one of the best ways to prompt students to reexamine their assumption that the Bolsheviks lacked popular support in the autumn of 1917 was to introduce them to the book at an early stage of the course. The book serves a similar purpose today—but the assumption that it forces students to reexamine is often that the Bolsheviks had overwhelming popular support and an indisputable mandate. It is difficult for even the most partisan reader to reject Radkey's evidence and his balanced, fair-minded discussion of its significance.

This achievement is the more impressive because, as those who know Oliver Radkey will testify, he is a man of strong opinions and convictions, not by any means a natural nonpartisan. Bolsheviks stand very low in Radkey's personal estimation. Socialist intellectuals of all stripes (Russian and otherwise) stand not much higher. His admiration and sympathy are reserved for peasants, particularly such economically independent and/or rebellious ones as those who are the subject of his book *The Unknown Civil War in Russia: A Study of the Green Movement in the Tambov Region, 1920–1921* (Stanford, 1976).

In *Russia Goes to the Polls*, Radkey has meticulously incorporated all additional data on election returns that have appeared in Soviet publications or otherwise become accessible since *The Election* was published. These data broaden the picture consid-

erably, providing important insights on the political configura-
tions in various parts of the empire. Indeed, Radkey's tables,
which break the electorate down into 80 electoral districts (71
districts in 14 regions plus 2 metropolitan districts and 7 districts
for the armies and fleets), can become almost compulsive reading
for any historian who works in the imperial or Soviet period.

Consider the variety of political, social, and ethnic relations
conveyed by the regional election returns. In Ufa electoral district, Moslem parties won 41 percent of the vote (32 percent to
parties of the left, 9 percent to the right), and a local Bashkir
party ("Turkic but not Tatar," in Radkey's designation) won 14
percent. In Kazan, another Volga region, the result was similar,
except that it was a Chuvash rather than a Bashkir party that
took almost a quarter of the vote. In the Amur-Maritime region,
independent peasant parties, with 27 percent of the vote, topped
both the SRs (23 percent) and the Bolsheviks (20 percent). In the
Siberian region of Tobolsk, by contrast, the SRs walked away
with 79 percent of the total votes, with one of only two undivided
Social Democratic lists of this election managing less than 3
percent.

Consider also the portents for the future that can be read in
these figures. In the Don Cossack electoral district of the Southeast, for example, Cossack parties received 45 percent of a total
vote of 1.4 million, while the Bolsheviks received a mere 15
percent. Small wonder that the Soviet regime was to encounter
severe difficulties in this region, not only during the Civil War
but when it came to collectivization a decade later. At the same
time, another kind of portent of the future, relevant even for far-
flung provincial regions remote from Bolshevik influence in
1917, can be read in the electoral returns. Out of the 4.1 million
votes recorded from the armed forces, 1.7 million went to the
Bolsheviks. The soldiers and sailors who cast those votes were
shortly to be dispersed throughout Russia, bringing home to Kazan, Ufa, and Khabarovsk the political attitudes and experience
gained in their military service.

The electoral showing of the parties Radkey labels "religious and/or rightist" was dismal. It is hard not to feel a twinge of sympathy for those 2,018 voters in the revolutionary Baltic Fleet who voted for an officers' party. Yet even here there is considerable interest in the regional spread of the votes. Monarchist parties made no significant showing anywhere but in an old Black Hundreds stronghold, the Kiev electoral district, where they won 48,758 votes (3 percent). (As a kind of dialectical antithesis, one notes that Zionist parties in Kiev, Volynia, and Minsk took 6 to 7 percent of the popular vote, with Kherson rising to 14 percent.) Both Orthodox and Old Believer parties made their best showing in Nizhni Novgorod (respectively 8 percent and 3 percent of total vote) and Perm electoral districts (4 percent and 3 percent). The Orthodox also made a showing in Kostroma (Central Industrial region), where there was no Old Believer electoral presence, and the Old Believer parties did the same in Altai, where they had no Orthodox competition. Landowners' parties (in Radkey's category of "special-interest groups") were strongest in Tambov, Saratov, and Chernigov, with a little over 1 percent of the vote in each.

The eye is caught by such curiosities as the 885 voters of the Taurida electoral district (including the Crimea) who gave their allegiance to a party of the Molokan sect. On the other end (one presumes) of the political spectrum, the League of Women Voters mustered a total of 7,676 votes, 2,366 of them in Pskov electoral district and 5,310 in the city of Petrograd.

Radkey collected these figures through years of patient, painstaking, even obsessive detective work. I can give some personal account of this process. I remember an urgent quest one Christmas Eve for an Austin resident fluent in Armenian, as Radkey had just acquired a book in Armenian and he suspected that one of its tables might possibly shed light on the elusive election returns of the Transcaucasus. (Alas, it was a false lead. The table turned out to be about damage to Armenian property inflicted by the Turks during World War I.) On another occasion, I made notes in the Academy of Sciences' library in

Leningrad from the last issue ever published of an obscure news-paper from Pskov, which Radkey knew to be the only extant source recording the vote for the League of Women Voters. When I returned to Texas with the Pskov data, Radkey informed me triumphantly that this was the conclusion of a search that had begun "on May 19, 1936" (or some such date)—more than half a century earlier!

In Part Two of this volume, Radkey has modified his earlier conclusions in two respects. In the first place, he feels more strongly than he did before that the large SR vote was "soft." He now attaches greater significance to the unofficial lists presented by peasants in competition with the official SR lists, which the SR-dominated electoral commissions usually ignored or refused to confirm on some technicality. Peasants, he concludes, were "becoming restive under SR domination." The SR intellectuals, for their part, were showing their "latent hostility . . . toward independent political activity on the part of peasants."

In the second place, Radkey feels that in The *Election* he may have been inclined to underplay the significance of the Bolshevik vote, making "certain concessions" (which he now regrets) to the argument made both on the Right and in SR circles that the Bolsheviks' strength was unimportant and ephemeral, destined to disappear with the self-demobilization of the army. He argues now that the support for the Bolsheviks was real, reflecting the "thoroughly revolutionary" temper of the country. Its non-emphemeral nature is confirmed by the outcome of the Civil War, which the Reds after all won and the Whites, despite Allied support, lost. He writes that the election "reflected no momentary aberration on the part of the population but rather the broadness, depth, and power of the revolution set off against the weakness of its foes." Then, in a summation that deserves to be pondered by all students of the revolution, he concludes that it showed two things: on the one hand, "that the Bolsheviks were strong"; on the other, that they were "not strong enough to govern democratically, even had they so desired."

It will be noted that Radkey describes the evolution of his study over the four decades since *The Election* appeared without reference to any historian but the unfortunate (in this context) Soviet researcher L. M. Spirin. That is characteristic of him, as Radkey is a scholar of deeply independent bent who does not pay a great deal of attention to the opinions of others. Yet, for all his Texan individualism, *Russia Goes to the Polls* must be read as an important contribution to contemporary scholarly debate. In the context of the work of such scholars as Alexander Rabinowitch, William G. Rosenberg, and, most recently, Vladimir Brovkin on popular support for the Bolsheviks in 1917 and the subsequent fluctuations of Russian political attitudes, *Russia Goes to the Polls* turns out to be in many respects *more* relevant to the preoccupations of American Soviet historians in 1990 than *The Election* was in 1950. At the same time, it is one of those rare scholarly works that strike us as the definitive account of a particular historical episode.

In 1987 the University of Texas, where Oliver Radkey taught from 1939 till his retirement forty years later, honored him by creating a professorship in his name, which it has been my privilege to hold for several years. This book may perhaps encourage a younger generation of American Soviet historians, sometimes accused of disrespect for their elders, to reassess the contribution of the postwar generation of scholars that established American Soviet studies. We sometimes write as if that cohort contained no historians. But Oliver Radkey, who belonged to it, is a historian par excellence. We will have a hard time matching his achievement.

SHEILA FITZPATRICK

Austin, Texas

PREFACE

THE VOLUME OF literature that has been published on the revolution of 1917, particularly on its course in the provinces, during the decades that have passed since the appearance of the first version of this study in 1950 gave hope that a mass of new material would now be available. The hope has not been realized. Information has continued to be scarce, scattered, and replete with imperfections. The subject of the election of 1917 is not taboo in the Soviet Union but there is an obvious bending away from it lest a false step be made. Soviet writers sometimes simply ignore it, sometimes brush it aside to concentrate on happenings in the network of soviets; when an occasional scholar has seriously taken it in hand, the practice has been not to venture beyond the confines of Lenin's analysis, based on N. V. Sviatitski's statistics. Very seldom has an attempt been made to adduce new information or to fill out or free from error what already is known; very seldom do the canons of historical research prevail over the stereotyped procedure prescribed from above.

Even so, the accumulation of bits of information over a long period of time can yield results. Enough has been done to justify a revision, from both the numerical and the interpretive standpoints. The earlier study registered 41,686,876 votes in 60 of the 80 electoral districts, compared with a total of 36,257,960 in 54 districts compiled by Sviatitski in 1918. This book lifts the total to 44,218,555 in 70 districts, some of them represented by only a thin vote, it is true. It has been possible to bring the Socialist Revolutionary (SR) strength over the 16 million mark, the Bolshevik over the 10 million, the Constitutional Democratic (Kadet) over the 2 million. Nothing availed to bring the Menshevik vote even to 1.5 million. Joint lists prevent a precise figure from being assigned to the Ukrainian following but it would be well over 5 million. Turko-Tatar strength approaches 2.5 million, and that of diverse nationalities is close to 2 million, or considerably more, depending on how Georgian Menshevism is classified (here it is classified as Menshevik, but if the election had been held even a year later, it would have had to be Georgian national). A noteworthy achievement is now the ability to present complete returns from nine more districts, several of them—Kazan, Saratov, Kharkov, and the Baltic Fleet—of preeminent importance. Success from scratch was attained in the case of Kaluga and the Chinese Eastern Railroad: full returns, where before we had nothing at all. Contrary to any reasonable expectation, Kharkov proved so unyielding a stumbling block that a search beginning in 1934 and extending to 1986—fifty-two years of sustained though intermittent effort—was required to overcome it. These nine districts join twenty-eight others that were complete at the time of the earlier survey to form a solid statistical foundation for this study. In addition a number of others have been filled out short of completion, some so close to it that they may now be pronounced satisfactory despite the few remaining defects; examples are the provinces of Perm, Taurida, Moscow, and Yenisei. There remain the stone-wall districts, impervious to investigation. A few have developed fissures. Merely to have a quarter of a million votes from Bessarabia seems a major achievement after so many years of frustration.

Compiling as complete a record as possible of this unique event in Russian history has been a primary objective, but by no means the only one. A second has been accuracy, and it has not been sacrificed to the first. High standards have been set and rigidly adhered to. Anything in the way of estimates, projections, or surmises has been rejected even though the result is to drive down the total rather than augment it. Likewise in the case of figures seemingly plausible and quite possibly valid, yet for some reason subject to doubt, the decision has been not to accept them unless they are confirmed by a source independent of the one in question. A strong prejudice has operated against figures ending in three zeros—against rounding off, in other words, or against approximation. Three such figures appear in the tables and they are there for good reason. One of them, the Bolshevik vote in Simbirsk province, is the subject of comment in Part Two. Notwithstanding the quest for accuracy, I am in no position to claim infallibility for my findings. I am only too conscious of the many defects that have been detected in the sources to think that none have escaped detection. A flawless record of this election will never be made; the circumstances were too adverse.

A chronic source of trouble is the question whether a town has been included in the uezd of which it is the center, if, as is often the case, the vote for a district has to be assembled from its parts. It is indispensable to know how many electoral commissions there were, particularly the number of town commissions, for an important town would have its own commission and be reported separately. An ordinary uezd center would not be so favored, and the chances of confusion go up steeply. They are there in any event. For years I could not put together the reports from Moscow province. The elements would not match. Finally in idle desperation I added in the figure for Orekhovo-Zuevo apart from its uezd and things fell into place as though by magic. Orekhovo-Zuevo was not listed as having a commission of its own and so should have been included in the report for its uezd. But it had a commission, just the same.

An even worse source of trouble is to establish whether the garrison vote has been included in the vote for a city. Garrisons did not have their own commissions but they had separate polling stations and so usually the result is totaled up and announced in a bloc. But whether it has then been fused with the civilian vote or left segregated is the question that bedevils the investigator. A classic example of the confusion that may arise is seen in Sviatitski's addition of the garrison vote of Moscow to a total that already contains it. And Sviatitski is a primary source, he was the statistician of the SRs and later of Lenin, and was himself elected deputy from Kharkov province. Blessed are the reports that state clearly what is included and what is not. In their absence vigilance is enjoined upon the investigator, who may or may not be responsible for mistakes that are made; they may simply inhere in the subject.

My third objective has been to apply the first two objectives, fullness and accuracy, to the competing lists of candidates with a view toward rescuing from oblivion those that have been slighted and testing the fairness of the conventional classification to which they have been subjected. This objective requires going around both Sviatitski and Soviet sources to the bedrock of information contained in the publications of the All-Russian Electoral Commission, a source as rewarding as it is rare. Interesting discoveries have been the result. Both the SR spokesman and his Soviet adversaries have a pronounced aversion to acknowledging independent action on the part of peasants; common to both is the view that peasants must be under tutelage, if not their own, then that of landowners (for connotations of this term, see "LO" under "Notes and Abbreviations" in Part Three). And so they are at pains to represent a peasant's list as a landowner's list, concealing both the truth and their own discomfort. Landowners, for their part, are not averse to adopting some peasant designation in order to broaden their appeal. Similarly with candidacies described as reactionary by Sviatitski, or Black Hundred in Soviet accounts, that turn out to be merely Orthodox. An erroneous classification of some magnitude is the designation as Socialist Revolutionary of certain independent lists put forth by nationality groups that may have had some tenuous tie with Populism but differed sharply with the main-line SRs over burning issues of the day, such as the war, the future of federalism in what had been the Russian empire, and land distribution as between Russian and native populations. The task of classification is a demanding one; it is essential to consult the literature of the commissions, central and provincial, something that was not done for the earlier publication, and to draw on whatever local information may be available.

The results have been eminently satisfactory. It has been possible to identify nearly all lists consigned to oblivion or buried in catchall columns, and in numerous instances to provide them with classifications more in accord with their nature. Whereas in respect to the votes cast this book registers merely further progress toward completeness, the treatment of what was voted on has achieved completeness. This latter endeavor has been powerfully aided by the work of the electoral commissions prior to the election; the former endeavor has suffered grievously from the void created by the Soviet government when, determined not to let the loss of the election lead to the loss of power, it struck down the central commission, causing the network below it to resemble an organism without a central nervous system. Aside from very valuable early returns, therefore, the election results have had to be assembled from dispersed and inferior sources. The success in reclaiming lists with their support from the undivided residue may seem slight when the total in the "Unclassified" column in the appendix to the 1950 work (Part One of this volume, pp. 78–80) is compared with the total in the "Residue" column of Table 1 in Part Three (pp. 148–149); actually, there is a big difference because the work of reclamation from the earlier residue has been obscured or offset in the total by the shifting of joint lists into the residue (column 11 of Table 1) of this book. Nothing can be done with joint lists; they cannot be dissolved into their component elements, they belong in the residue,[*] and should have been there from the start. Of the 1,932,726 votes in the current residue, 1,428,730 represent joint lists. The remainder represents a failure of this study—votes that were cast but that cannot be distributed because they are lumped together in the only sources available. They number many fewer, however, than in the work of 1950.

---

[*]Except when they are made up of two components in adjoining columns; then such a figure is made to straddle these two columns, is independent of both, and must be incorporated separately into the grand total.

This book consists of three parts.

Part One is *The Election to the Russian Constituent Assembly of 1917*, reprinted just as it is, without revision or amendment. It has unity and a life of its own. It also has assertions that need to be modified and some factual errors. But it reflects the state of knowledge in 1950 and still serves quite well as a lead-in to the subject. The money saved by a simple reprint can better be spent in publishing without abridgment the new and elaborate tabulations that are the heart of the new volume. I have preferred to spend my time on new ground in quest of further information rather than on pulling apart what has already been done—a disheartening enterprise and boring besides. Nor is it imperative, as an example will show. It was an error to state in 1950 that no election was held in Russian Turkestan (or Central Asia—really west-central Asia). Since then I have found what appear to be complete returns for Semirechie, a remote region in the northeast, against the Chinese frontier, and a Soviet historian has produced seemingly valid figures for Uralsk province, in the northwest. Sporadic voting took place elsewhere but the votes were not assembled and may not even have been counted, such was the state of disorganization in the turmoil of the time. Yet it is still as true today as it was then that the election failed in most of Turkestan and it is still true that this failure prevented the nationality vote from exceeding the Bolshevik show of strength or even equaling it. Thus the error is not of great consequence. Finally, this matter and others of similar nature are set right in Parts Two and Three.

Part Two supplements the material in Part One. It is the product of increased knowledge and greater maturity, it provides new insights and corrects certain misconceptions, it reexamines certain fundamental aspects of the subject and modifies or scraps certain conclusions, it deals *in extenso* with the difficulties of the study and appraises its successes and failures. It discloses the relationship to other compilations (there are only two). Those who are in need of background may read Part One; those who are familiar with the earlier work or who have background for 1917 may go directly to Parts Two and Three, where they will find what is new and what has been amended.

Part Two is a series of free essays, unencumbered by citations. An attempt to include them would have choked the flow of the narrative and the analysis as effectively as the proliferation of water plants in the southern Sudan chokes the flow of the Nile. A study dependent on a little here and a little there from a broad field and requiring the inspection of a still greater number of sources that yield nothing at all does not lend itself to citations or a formal bibliography. Part Two pays attention in a general way to bibliography, and some specific works of significance are mentioned in the text. And that will have to do. Not that there is no systematic record of what has been done. Upon my death, the master cards and the ancillary cards and all the other assorted materials, some of considerable value, that bear on the subject and have been assembled over a period of fifty-two years go into the archives of the Hoover Institution, there to be preserved as the bedrock of this research.

Part Three opens with a note about the more technical aspects of the statistical tables that follow. The condensed tabulation of the vote (Table 1) is followed by expanded tabulations (Tables 2–5) that lay out the record of the election in its entirety. In these tables one can for the first time find a comprehensive presentation of the vote received by lesser parties and groups as well as by major ones. There are no dumping columns, no catchall categories, to which the lesser lists are consigned and which obscure a part of the election in accordance with SR bias or Soviet dogma, as in the other two compilations of any consequence. The second unique feature of Part Three is the much greater attention paid the identity of the contesting parties or groups with a view toward their proper classification or reclassification. To repeat, a total vote of over 44 million, despite strict standards requiring reduction as well as addition, rejection as well as acceptance, is an approach to completeness; but the inclusion of less obvious lists and their proper identification is the achievement of completeness. In these respects the tables leave behind any other record of the election. They are, in fact, the main part of this study.

A word about what is excluded. There are no percentages to obstruct the view of the figures. The last column of the general tabulation (Table 1) gives the total vote for each district, insofar as it is available; the reader can relate a figure to it and get the percentage. Nor are there any separate tables for towns or garrisons, aside from the fact that the two metropolitan areas constitute districts in their own right, that the thin returns for the Steppe district are for Omsk and outlying settlements, and that Vladivostok is treated in Part Two. General comment on the town vote will be found in Part One (Chapter V). Towns and garrisons have received a disproportionate amount of attention in Soviet sources, and for a simple reason—they show Bolshevism to better advantage. This work stresses results as a whole— all elements are represented, including the peasantry. And if it be contended that the triumphant march of Bolshevism proves the irrelevance of the peasant vote, it may be answered that the election foretold what would happen if its lessons were spurned; what happened was surprising only in its magnitude and engulfed even the triumphant party, reducing it by the end of 1938 to a hunk of bloody meat, bereft of members of independent spirit with thought of the population beneath it, and stacked with sycophants and crawlers.

OLIVER H. RADKEY

Austin, Texas
April 1987

ACKNOWLEDGMENTS

I HAVE ALWAYS preferred to work alone. In this instance, however, I have had a good deal of help, and so it is fitting to express gratitude where gratitude is due.

The quest for the results of the election of 1917 began long ago, sixteen years after the event, on the proceeds of a traveling fellowship from Harvard University, in the Russian Archives Abroad under the Czechoslovak Ministry of Foreign Affairs, with the aid of three older friends of cherished memory, Dr. Jan Slavík, director; Dr. A. F. Iziumov, head of the Archival Division; and S. P. Postnikov, head of the Book Division and editor of *Delo Naroda* in 1917 (died it is not known when or where).

At first the study of the election was a by-product of a dissertation on the Socialist Revolutionary Party; later it branched off from that line of investigation, assumed independent status, and became an end in itself. Its preparation was made possible by financial aid from the Hoover Library under the guidance of Harold H. Fisher and by assistance from the librarian Philip T. McLean, who from the beginning set things on the right course. The publication of its first version by Harvard University Press was arranged by two friends and well-wishers, Michael Karpovich and Oscar Handlin. I owe much to Professors Fisher (died 1975), Karpovich (died 1959), and Handlin, without whose efforts on my behalf the study would have gotten nowhere.

The two succeeding directors of what is now the Hoover Institution, Easton Rothwell and Glenn Campbell, and Associate Director Witold Sworakowski (died 1979) have continued to further my work in many ways, above all by providing a base of operations not less pleasant than profitable. Their friendship has been a sustaining factor through the years. The reference librarians Ruth Perry, Arlene Paul, Hilja Kukk, and Linda

Wheeler have never failed to honor requests that all too often were costly in time and difficult of execution. Among other members of the staff, words of appreciation are due my friends Barbara Lazarev, Helen Pashin, and Boris Dybenski (died 1985) for their many kindnesses.

Staff personnel of other libraries have contributed significantly to the gathering of information. At the University of California in Berkeley, Helen Balashova of the Slavic exchange program succeeded in getting from the Soviet Union a number of sources with promising titles that could not be found in this country. My former student Molly Molloy, now at Arizona State University, had previously worked in the same direction, and their friend and my daughter, Ingrid Radkey, has given valuable assistance in regard to bibliographical matters and new library techniques. Two enterprising and highly competent librarians of the interlibrary service at the University of Texas, Patricia Thomas and Christina Hanson, produced results beyond expectations in extracting from the Soviet Union certain publications of early date that would hardly have been entrusted to the mail in this country.

There remain individuals unconnected with academic institutions who have volunteered their assistance out of friendship or because of interest in the subject. An uncommon case is that of a New York businessman, H. Emmons Raymond, who was captivated by the earlier monograph and went quite deeply into the matter, drawing up tables of his own, consulting with me, making suggestions of merit, and even learning to read the Russian language. He has furnished me with a copy of an extremely rare and indispensable source, Sviatitski's book on the election, published in Moscow in 1918, which is not alluded to in Soviet publications. As they refer only to his earlier and much inferior chapter in a collaborative work (*God russkoi revoliutsii*), one is led to wonder whether Sviatitski's book may have been torn from the press, as later a history of the peasants' soviets in 1917 assuredly was. Yet 1918 seems to be early for such action against the socialist opposition. At any rate, one copy found its way to France, whence came Raymond's duplication and gift to me. All honor, then, to this businessman of scholarly proclivities; he has performed a signal service.

No one has contributed more to the fund of information for this venture than my former student and younger friend Charles A. Duval, who during a stay in the Soviet Union (1979–80) procured from leads I had given him the definitive returns from four major districts. The search was made at his insistence, not at my urging, in several weeks of devoted labor, with a professional competence that promised much for the future. But there was no future, for he was killed the following year. I owe him the province of Saratov, long sought after and ardently desired as the hearth of agrarian revolution in 1905 and, even more, as the home ground of Social Revolutionism and so connected with the earliest beginnings of my research. His contribution to this work was one of his last actions; his biography of J. M. Sverdlov remains unpublished.

A matter of lesser though still profound regret concerns historians in the Soviet Union worthy of being called historians. There are some. In going through accounts of 1917 without number, amid an ocean of Communist claptrap, I from time to time have found islets of true scholarship. Some of the inhabitants of these islets ought to be mentioned even in this brief acknowledgment. Yet in noting their existence and commending their work, I have judged it advisable not to mention their names. One more manifestation of the evil fate that overhangs this subject.

A word of appreciation is due my friend Jim J. Davis for presenting the tables in a form easy to look upon. Much patience and considerable skill were required to achieve this result.

Finally, I thank Professor Sheila Fitzpatrick for the inestimable service of offering to include this work in the series of which she is co-editor for Cornell University Press, Studies in Soviet History and Society, thus obviating the whole wearisome process of seeking a publisher, a process so irksome to me that I might at my age have decided not to go through with it. I am also grateful to John G. Ackerman, editor-in-chief of Cornell University Press, for his enthusiastic agreement with her wish. Both editors have been most considerate. Professor Fitzpatrick's role has not been restricted to publication, of transcendent importance though that be. She has also added in significant measure to the fund of information upon which the book is based.

I have now made the acknowledgments. I acknowledge no laws of history. But of one truth I am convinced—that nature keeps things more or less in balance. In this instance the assistance, kindness, and contributions I have here set forth supply the balance to an enterprise condemned in advance to be beset by difficulties and weighed down by disappointments.

O. H. R.

PART ONE

The Election to the Russian
Constituent Assembly of 1917

CHAPTER I

THE SETTING

NO DEFINITIVE STUDY of the election to the All-Russian Constituent
Assembly in the fall and winter of 1917 has yet been made. Today,
on the thirtieth anniversary of that mournful occasion when more
than forty million votes were cast in vain, it seems less than ever
likely that such a study will or can be made, for the obstacles that
lie in the way are so numerous and forbidding that even Soviet
investigators, with all the advantages that location and official
favor can give, have despaired of the task and have consigned it
to oblivion.[1]

Yet an attempt at reconstruction of what took place will always
have historical validity, if only because this is the one real election in the experience of the Russian people — real, that is, in the
sense that it was a fundamentally free election, contested by definitely organized and sharply divergent parties, on the basis of universal, equal, direct, and secret suffrage. It is true that it was
held during one of the great crises of Russian history, and hence
reflected a mood less stable than that which would have prevailed
in normal times; yet merely to record the will of a great people at
a crucial stage of its development is to preserve something of

[1] Tsentrarkhiv, Arkhiv Oktiabrskoi Revoliutsii (hereinafter cited as AOR),
1917 g. v dokumentakh i materialakh, ed. M. N. Pokrovski and Ia. A.
Iakovlev: *Vserossiiskoe Uchreditelnoe Sobranie*, ed. I. S. Malchevski, (Moscow-Leningrad, 1930), p. xxviii. As further evidence of the difficulties encountered, the author of the present study may cite his own experience. In
assembling the materials used here he found it necessary to draw on the re-
sources of no less than six widely spaced libraries: the Russian Archives
Abroad in Prague, the Marx-Engels-Lenin Institute at Moscow, the Moscow
Public Library, the Bibliothèque de la Guerre at Vincennes, the Widener
Library of Harvard University, and the Hoover Library in California. Of
these only the Widener Library could have been dispensed with; each of the
others contained indispensable information not available in the other four.
Finally, there is certain valuable information that is not to be found in any
of these libraries.

enduring value, quite apart from the disclosure of certain tend-
encies in the vast Eurasian empire which are in no sense transitory
but are of permanent significance. How, then, can the obscurity
that has surrounded this historic event be explained?

The abortive nature of the ill-fated assembly is one reason for
the neglect of the election which produced it. Lenin dissolved the
Constituent Assembly by force after a single session on January 5,
1918,[2] amid the plaudits, open or secret, of both the extremes of
Russian political life. Of more fateful significance was the fact
that while the democratic parties heaped opprobrium upon him
for this act of despotism, their following showed little inclination [3]
to defend an institution which the Russian people had ceased to
regard as necessary to the fulfillment of its cherished desires. For
the Constituent Assembly, even before it had come into existence,
had been caught in a back-eddy of the swiftly flowing stream of
revolutionary developments and no longer commanded the interest
and allegiance of the general population which alone could have
secured it against a violent death.

Even had its existence not been so swiftly terminated, however,
the greater interest in the assembly would not necessarily have
guaranteed a clearer record of its origins. The election, or rather
the elections, had taken place under the most unfavorable circumstances. Quite apart from the vastness of Russia and the general
unfamiliarity with democratic procedure, the mere fact that the
election was held less than nine months after one revolution and
less than three weeks after another rendered the task of administration exceedingly difficult. Set for November 12–14 (25–27),
the vote came off as scheduled in most of the country, but in a
number of districts preparations had not been completed and post-
ponement was necessary, with the result that the balloting was

[2] January 18 by the Western calendar. For the sake of convenience, and
also because it continued to be official until 1918, the Old Style has been
retained throughout this study.

[3] At least at this time. Later on, in the first stages of the civil war, the
SR's whipped up considerable popular sentiment against the Bolsheviks on
the grounds that the Soviet government had violated the will of the people
in dissolving the Constituent Assembly.

strung out over a period of three months and, in some cases, never took place at all.[4] The returns came in unevenly, for the electoral machinery remained in the hands of commissions appointed by the Provisional Government after that regime itself had been supplanted by the Bolsheviks; as a consequence, unity of administration was lost in the clash of authority. The system of communications had become disrupted, especially the telegraph, making it difficult for the *uezd* [5] electoral commissions to report to the district commissions,[6] not to speak of the difficulties encountered by the latter in communicating with the All-Russian Commission on Affairs Pertaining to the Election of the Constituent Assembly in Petrograd. And even if the results were known locally, that does not mean that record of them exists today, for precisely at the time they were being announced, the Bolshevik campaign against the press reached its height and newspapers were being suppressed right and left (in a double sense).[7] Add to these factors the dreadful incubus of a long and exhausting war

[4] N. V. Sviatitski, *Kogo russkii narod izbral svoimi predstaviteliami?* (Moscow, n.d.), pp. 3–4. See also below, p. 6.

[5] The term *uezd* has been retained here as its nearest equivalent, the word "county," somehow does not fit. On the other hand, *guberniia* will be rendered by "province" and *volost* by "canton." In the Russian administrative system, the largest unit was the province, consisting of a number of *uezds*, each of which in turn was subdivided into cantons, and each of these into villages. The electoral set-up followed roughly the same lines, the largest unit being known as *okrug* (district) rather than *guberniia* (province). In most instances, however, "district" and "province" were one and the same.

[6] "Chleny Uchreditelnago Sobraniia ot Saratovskoi gubernii," *Vestnik Privolzhskago Kraia*, no. 2 (December 16, 1917). This editorial cites the example of Kamyshin *uezd*. Another type of trouble in the same province is indicated in the following telegram, sent by the chairman of the Kuznetsk *uezd* commission on November 22 to the district commission in Saratov: "Ransacking of state liquor warehouse began in town today. Great deal of drunkenness. Population in panic. Plundering of banks and merchants impending. Work of *uezd* commission halted" (quoted in *Saratovskii Vestnik*, no. 251, November 23, 1917).

[7] As an illustration, the two papers cited in the foregoing footnote are actually one. The *Saratovskii Vestnik* was suppressed and had to reappear under a new title. Then it, too, was suppressed. Later on the Bolsheviks did better — one act of suppression was enough to close down a paper under any guise.

which bore down upon the Russian state and people with crushing weight, and the further devastating experience of the civil war that lay ahead, with all the loss entailed in respect to local records, and one will begin to understand why the facts concerning a general election, held in a great country as recently as 1917, should today be so largely unknown.

Only three investigations of fundamental significance to the study of this election have been published. Though thirty years have gone by, the basic work is still that of the Socialist Revolutionary deputy and electoral statistician, N. V. Sviatitski, who tabulated the returns, insofar as they were available to him, and analyzed them in reasonably objective fashion.[8] Lenin followed with a commentary on the election based upon the study of Sviatitski, which he took over without change as far as statistics were concerned, neither adding to them nor questioning their validity. Naturally, Lenin's interpretation was his own and differs markedly from that of Sviatitski, but his point of view was by no means as biased as one might expect, for he conscientiously sought in the figures the lessons they contained for his party, whether flattering or otherwise, and his deductions constitute a thoroughgoing and penetrating analysis of the results.[9] Years later, under the auspices of the Archives of the October Revolution, a study appeared which contains the stenographic report of the proceedings of the Constituent Assembly and sheds some further light, in the annotations and introduction, upon the election itself. The contribution is a modest one, however, since the original

---

[8] "Itogi vyborov vo Vserossiiskoe Uchreditelnoe Sobranie (predislovie)," *God russkoi revoliutsii (1917–1918g.g.)*: *Sbornik statei* (Moscow, 1918), pp. 104–119. This article was expanded somewhat and appeared in book form under the same title, *Itogi vyborov vo Vserossiiskoe Uchreditelnoe Sobranie* (Moscow, 1918). Both are rare. Lenin used the article, not the book, as material for his study. Sviatitski also published a pamphlet (no. 86 in the SR series) in answer to Bolshevik charges as to the counterrevolutionary composition of the assembly; this pamphlet is cited above, note 4. He also wrote short analyses for the *Delo Naroda* during the voting period. Sviatitski's writings have a mild SR slant.

[9] "Vybory v Uchreditelnoe Sobranie i diktatura proletariata," *Sochineniia* (2nd ed.; Moscow-Leningrad, 1930–1932), XXIV (1919), 631–649.

project of compiling a full set of returns which would supersede those of Sviatitski could not be carried through, the tangible gain being restricted to returns from four electoral districts which are missing in the earlier tabulation (Don Region, Stavropol, Orenburg, and the Transcaucasus). The editors also announced that they had been able to go beyond Sviatitski in a number of instances where his information was incomplete or inaccurate, but they did not publish their work of revision, simply incorporating it into the totals for the country at large.[10]

This is an unfortunate circumstance, for the present writer has also been able to improve the statistics of Sviatitski at a number of points, yet has no way of knowing what degree of coincidence may exist between his figures and those of the Soviet investigation. Consequently, there is no possibility of drawing all the information together and presenting totals for the country which would be definitive, even so far as the present status of research is concerned. Entire electoral districts are still missing, but in three cases, at least, the writer has succeeded in unearthing returns for districts which appear neither in Sviatitski's list nor in the Soviet supplement.[11] One of these is the Podolia district[12] in the Ukraine.[13]

[10] AOR, *Vserossiiskoe Uchreditelnoe Sobranie*, p. xxviii. They were able to verify his figures for 21 of the 55 districts included in the tabulation.

[11] See below, p. 12.

[12] Here electoral district and province are one, as is usually the case, so that a large and populous area is involved.

[13] *Robitnicha Gazeta* (organ of the central committee of the Ukrainian Social Democratic Party), no. 222 (January 6, 1918). Podolia will serve as an illustration of how difficult it is to assemble data pertaining to the election. Sviatitski not only did not have the returns but did not even know whether the voting had taken place; the blame he places on the "war" between the Bolsheviks and the Rada (*Itogi vyborov*, p. 38). The Ukrainian newspaper in which I found the figures states that the election was held on December 3–5, 1917, and that a total of 741,064 votes were cast in 9 of the 12 *uezds*, the other 3 not reporting. Yet if the vote as given for each party list is added up, the total is 830,260, indicating perhaps that one or more of the missing *uezds* had come in. The newspaper makes no attempt to explain the discrepancy. Later numbers contain no further information; the account was published on the day of the dissolution of the Constituent Assembly, and the whole matter appears subsequently to have become a dead issue.

No returns have yet been found for the Kaluga and Bessarabia districts of European Russia, nor for the three Far Eastern districts of Kamchatka, Iakutsk, and the Chinese Eastern Railroad, although balloting took place in each and the names of the victorious candidates are known.[14] Except for the city of Ekaterinodar, no election was held in the Kuban–Black Sea district of the North Caucasus, nor in the Terek–Daghestan area, and the same is true of all ten of the districts in Central Asia; approximately one hundred seats were thus left vacant in the Constituent Assembly.[15]

Bearing in mind these gaps in our knowledge, and remembering also that only partial returns are available for a number of districts, we can nevertheless obtain a clear picture of the results of the election. As we turn to them, the first thing that engages our attention is the multiplicity of parties vying for the favor of the Russian people. With some of these the Western reader is familiar; with others, he presumably is not. Only the basic distinctions can be pointed out here.

The socialist sector was divided into two camps — the Marxist and the Narodnik or Populist — and each of these was divided within itself. How the original Marxist movement, the Russian Social Democratic Workingmen's party, had fallen apart into the Menshevik and Bolshevik wings, and how these had grown further and further apart until by 1917 membership within the same party had become purely fictitious, is all a familiar story. It was a difference in temperament as much as in theory that divided the Russian Social Democrats: the Mensheviks were patient and cautious folk, who would not force the pace of events but would let the laws of capitalistic development work themselves

---

Even had interest been sustained, the wild times that ensued in the Ukraine might well have precluded the gathering of complete returns.

[14] See list of members of the Constituent Assembly in AOR, *Vserossiiskoe Uchreditelnoe Sobranie*, pp. 116–138, and foreword, pp. 114–115. The compilation of this list of more than 700 deputies is the most valuable service rendered by the Soviet investigation.

[15] M. V. Vishniak, *Vserossiiskoe Uchreditelnoe Sobranie* (Paris, 1932), pp. 91–92.

out. Nothing could be worse, they felt, than for a socialist party to come into power before society was ready for socialism, for in that case the socialist regime would be discredited in the eyes of its own followers in addition to encountering the desperate resistance of a still powerful propertied class. Until such time as capitalism had run its course in Russia and practically had fallen into the grave of its own digging, the Mensheviks would exploit the forms of the liberal state to build up the organization of the working class and educate it for the performance of its historic mission. Thus was their theory made to conform to their temperament. The Bolsheviks, on the other hand, were insurrectionary in spirit, conspiring to seize the power of state as the conscious vanguard of the proletariat and from that vantage ground to complete the organization of the toiling masses and bring in the socialist order of society.[16] Both groups were staunchly Marxist in ideology; Menshevism must not be confused with revisionism. If anything, the Bolsheviks were less hidebound and more given to experimentation than their rivals. The official line of the Menshevik Party lay decidedly to the left of the Majority Socialists in Germany, being comparable to that of the Austrian and Saxon Social Democrats.

The rival Narodnik or Populist school of socialism was nativist in inspiration and agrarian in emphasis. It held that Russia could arrive at socialism in her own way, building upon those hoary institutions and folk habits like the village commune which had

[16] In this connection a passage from Lenin's treatise on the election (p. 639) merits translation *in extenso*: "The opportunist gentlemen, among them the followers of Kautsky, are 'instructing' the people, in mockery of Marx's teaching, that the proletariat must first achieve a majority by means of universal suffrage, then on the basis of such a majority vote take over the government, and only then proceed to organize socialism on the foundation of this 'progressive' (others say 'pure') democracy. But we speak from the vantage-ground of Marxist doctrine *and the experience of the Russian Revolution* [italics are mine]: the proletariat must first overthrow the bourgeoisie and conquer *for itself* the power of state, then use this power — i.e., the dictatorship of the proletariat — as an instrument of its own class for the purpose of winning the sympathies of a majority of the toilers" (also quoted in Vishniak, p. 93*n*).

retarded or inhibited the development of a property consciousness on the part of the Russian people. In view of this fortuitous circumstance — fortuitous, that is, from the Narodnik viewpoint — Russia's society need not be subjected to the disintegrating influences of capitalist development or to the Marxist projection of the class war into the village.[17] It had broadened the Marxist concept of the class struggle by ranging the "toiling" peasantry (those who worked the soil without recourse to hired labor) and the "toiling" intelligentsia alongside the proletariat in the army of the exploited; in fact, it was much more concerned with the peasantry than with the proletariat. Its cardinal tenet was that "all the land should belong to all the people" — that is, that the usufruct (but not the ownership) of the land should be vested equally in those who worked it with their own hands. In simplest terms, the Narodniks were people who wanted to make a revolution in an overwhelmingly agrarian country and had to devise an ideology that would justify an appeal to what was by far the strongest subversive force in Tsarist Russia — the elemental discontent of the rural masses. Nothing was more certain than that this appeal would be made, and since the Marxists did not choose to make it, the Narodniks did. At the time of the first revolution (1905–1907) the Narodnik movement had split into two parties, the minority Popular Socialists drawing away from the majority Socialist Revolutionaries because of their aversion to the strident republicanism and taste for terrorism of the dominant faction. After the February Revolution in 1917 the Popular Socialists continued to be a very small though highly conscious group, while the Party of the Socialist Revolutionaries (PSR) swelled to enormous proportions.

Some salient features of this party — the largest in the country — may be pointed out for the benefit of the Western reader. The core of the PSR was the rural intelligentsia: the village scribes, the children of the priests, the employees of the *zemstvos* and coöperatives, and, above all, the village schoolteachers. The party's

---

[17] This the Narodniks abhorred above all else, desiring to preserve the solidarity of the peasantry, apart from the *kulak* element.

center of gravity lay not in the heart of Great Russia, in the region around Moscow, but to the southeast, in the black-earth zone and along the middle and lower Volga. The city of Saratov, sometimes called the "Athens of the Volga," had been associated with the earliest beginnings of the party and long had served it as a kind of intellectual capital. The SR ideology, partly, no doubt, because of its very vagueness, enjoyed tremendous popularity, and not only among the Great Russians: the Ukrainian intellectuals, intoxicated with the heady wine of nationalism, organized their own SR party with huge success, and along the middle Volga and between it and the Urals the movement spread to the native non-Russian populations, Finnish or Tatar, Orthodox or Mohammedan, assuming as it did so a nationalist or religious coloration.

It is conventional to regard all of the parties mentioned above as being socialistic, though the Marxists, for example, would deny that designation to the Narodniks. Turning now to the political camp which defended the institution of private property, we find the Constitutional Democrats, commonly known as "Kadets," standing virtually alone.[18] The conservative groups to the right of the Kadets in the Third and Fourth Dumas had been the products of a distorted electoral system and could not exist on the basis of universal, direct, and equal suffrage; they had simply vanished from the scene, being swallowed up for the most part by the Kadets.[19] The only rightist group with a truly popular following — the Union of Russian People — had either fallen apart as a result of the moral rottenness and material bankruptcy of the old regime or had been driven under cover to escape the fierce draught of the revolution. The scattered embers of this movement — one of whose slogans had been, "Beat the Jews and Save Russia!" — still glowed here and there on the Russian landscape and were by no means extinguished; the throne and the church still had their devoted adherents, and the Jews, their bitter enemies. But as an

[18] The Kadets' official name was *Narodnaia Svoboda* (People's Freedom) or *Partiia Narodnoi Svobody*.
[19] The chief of these conservative groups was the Octobrist. Others were the Progressive, Nationalist, and so on.

organized, All-Russian movement, the Union of Russian People had ceased to exist, even though locally it might contest the polls under various guises.

The Constitutional Democrats were a proud and influential party, numbering among their members the cream of the intellectual and business spheres of Russian society. Many university professors were Kadets, among them the party leader, P. N. Miliukov. A spirit of nationalism not untinged with imperialism pervaded the ranks of this party, and its leadership had seen in the war not so much a calamity as an opportunity to destroy the Teutonic hegemony over the Western and Southern Slavs and to acquire for Russia the Straits and Galicia. The party's inspiration was western, as was its orientation: it admired the institutions of France and Great Britain and fervently sustained the alliance against Germany and Austria. The party had not embraced republicanism until after the Tsar had lost his throne and, despite the semblance of unanimity achieved on that occasion,[20] undoubtedly contained within its ranks more than a few who preferred a constitutional monarchy. The Constitutional Democrats had their own scheme of land reform, under which the holdings of the peasantry would be enlarged through grants in perpetuity, the landowners being compensated by the state for their losses.[21]

----

[20] The VII party congress (March 25, 1917). See A. A. Kornilov, *Partiia Narodnoi Svobody (Istoricheskii ocherk)* (Petrograd, 1917), pp. 29–31, and "Partiia Narodnoi Svobody," *Sputnik izbiratelia v Uchreditelnoe Sobranie* (Petrograd, 1917), pp. 69–70. The Kadet historian writes as though monarchist sentiment had completely evaporated. Yet compare the attitude of Miliukov in the first days of the February Revolution. Thereafter, for some members at least, a republican solution became more a matter of expediency than an article of faith.

[21] These grants might be made either to societies or to individuals, as the peasants wished. The Kadets did not favor an enforced dissolution of the village commune. Their land program did not go as far toward establishing a regime of private property as one would expect. It occupied an intermediate position between the Stolypin legislation and the Narodnik program, the influence of which is palpably evident. See E. A. Morokhovets, *Agrarnye programmy rossiiskikh politicheskikh partii v 1917 godu* (Leningrad, 1929), pp. 141–153; text of program in *Programma Partii Narodnoi Svobody (Konstitutsionno-Demokraticheskoi)* (Petrograd, 1917), sec. vi, pp. 9–14.

These were the parties that fought the election to the Constituent Assembly. In the pages following, it is proposed, first, to set forth the results of the election, then to proceed to an analysis of these results, and thereafter to examine the conditions under which the balloting took place, with a view toward determining whether the results are valid or whether so much terrorism, intimidation, and knavery were practiced at the polls as to make the outcome of the election a caricature of the will of the Russian people. Finally, an attempt will be made to estimate the degree of consciousness of the voting public as it went to the polls.

CHAPTER II

ANALYSIS OF RETURNS FOR THE COUNTRY
AT LARGE

As ALREADY has been intimated, the electoral statistics are in a deplorable condition, being widely dispersed and shot through with inaccuracies and contradictions. In tabulating the votes it is necessary to give the totals for the country at large in three columns, none of which has any claim to completeness. The first contains the figures of Sviatitski, just as he gave them.[1] The second column represents the work of the Soviet Archives of the October Revolution, regarding which so little is said as to preclude verification or integration of the results.[2] The third column embodies the research of this author, who has taken the other two studies as a basis for his own, supplementing them wherever possible in one of two ways: either by incorporation of returns hitherto missing or by substitution of more complete or more accurate returns for those that were given.[3] In the case of four electoral districts — Olonets, Esthonia, Podolia, and the Baltic Fleet — it has been possible to produce returns where none were available to Sviatitski (three of these are likewise missing in the Soviet compilation, and the fourth — Esthonia — quite possibly is missing). In respect to a number of other electoral districts — Arkhangelsk, Tver, Samara, Saratov, Ienisei, Chernigov, Poltava,

---

[1] The column was made up on the basis of returns from 54 out of 79 districts. "Itogi vyborov," *God russkoi revoliutsii*, p. 106. Of these, two are pure guesswork and must be discarded (see below).

[2] Aside from the four new districts mentioned above. The results are based on 60 districts (*Vserossiiskoe Uchreditelnoe Sobranie*, p. 210, n. 13, and p. 211, n. 16). The editors accredit 55 districts to Sviatitski though he himself claims only 54. As they present only four new districts (p. xxviii), there are one or two others unaccounted for.

[3] The third column is based on 60 districts. Fifty-two of these are listed in Sviatitski's table, four in the AOR compilation, and four appear for the first time in this study.

Ekaterinoslav, and the Northern Front of the army — it has been possible to produce more complete returns than are found in Sviatitski, the differences resulting from substitution being especially large in the case of Tver, Saratov, Chernigov, Ekaterinoslav, and the Northern Front.[4] On the other hand, it has been necessary to reduce the totals given by Sviatitski through the deletion of two entire districts — Mogilev and the Caucasian Front — where he admits having resorted to pure guesswork in the absence of any returns.[5] The figures for the city of Moscow are cut down to eliminate duplication, since Sviatitski added the garrison vote to totals that already contained it.[6] In a number of other instances more detailed or more accurate returns have been substituted for those contained in his table.[7] On balance, the necessity of taking away from Sviatitski's totals as well as adding to them causes the work of revision appearing in the third column to seem less substantial than actually is the case.

The four new districts (Orenburg, Don, Stavropol, and the Transcaucasus) disclosed by Soviet research add no less than 4,298,854 votes to Sviatitski's total.[8] In the third column these

[4] For example, in the case of Saratov, Sviatitski divides a total of 390,211 votes among the parties, 196,400 for the SR's, 113,592 for the Bolsheviks, etc. Much more complete returns are used in the present study, the total vote being 954,559, of which the SR share was 564,250 and the Bolshevik 225,000. Even so, one *uezd* (Kamyshin) was still out. See the editorial, "Chleny Uchreditelnago Sobraniia ot Saratovskoi gubernii," in *Vestnik Privolzhskago Kraia*, no. 2 (December 16, 1917).

[5] *Itogi vyborov*, p. 25; "Itogi vyborov," *God russkoi revoliutsii*, pp. 106–107. 825,000 votes for Mogilev and 420,000 for the Caucasian Front are thus eliminated.

[6] This becomes apparent from a study and comparison of the accounts in the *Russkiia Vedomosti*, no. 257 (November 24, 1917), the *Russkoe Slovo*, no. 257 (November 24, 1917), and the *Izvestiia Moskovskago Soveta*, no. 213 (November 24, 1917).

[7] So for Vladimir, Moscow province, Kursk, Voronezh, Tambov, Tobolsk, Ienisei, Transbaikal region, Poltava, Kharkov, Taurida, and the Black Sea Fleet. Some of these changes are insignificant but others are substantial (e.g., a reduction of 65,250 in the total vote cast in the Taurida). An error of 20,000 was detected in Sviatitski's figures for the Transbaikal Region.

[8] AOR, *Vserossiiskoe Uchreditelnoe Sobranie*, p. xxviii. Unfortunately, there is no breakdown of the vote save for the SR, Bolshevik, and Kadet

have been included, along with an additional two and a half million votes — 2,569,650 to be exact — which represent the fruits of the present investigation, having been assembled independently either of Sviatitski or of the Archives of the October Revolution.

The table of returns for the whole country reveals clearly the over-all results of the election. Three weeks after the October Revolution, the Bolsheviks had signally failed to secure popular sanction for their seizure of power and had mustered only one-fourth of the electorate behind their banner. No amount of turning and twisting on their part could conceal their discomfiture. On the other hand, the various socialistic parties of all types and description had scored overwhelmingly — more than four-fifths of the people stood behind them, or at any rate had chosen their lists. But what kind of "socialism" was it that had triumphed? Mainly the Narodnik brand, to which the Marxists would deny the very name of socialism.[9] The peasants, as will be shown below, had given their suffrage to the Socialist Revolutionary party, traditionally associated in their minds with immediate expropriation of the land without compensation to the owners; that they themselves were not to have the land as private property meant very little to them, at least for the time being, since they had no concept of property comparable to that which had arisen

---

parties, the one exception being the Menshevik vote in Transcaucasia (*ibid.*, p. 213, n. 20). The Kadet vote for the Don Region is omitted, apparently by mistake. In all probability, however, it represents the discrepancy between the announced total and the sum of the votes for the two lists given plus the unclassified remainder. The Cossack vote is not given for either the Don or Orenburg districts, nor is the large Mohammedan or Armenian vote in the Transcaucasus reported separately. From another source, based on a total of 1,411,500 votes as against the official figure of 1,406,620, we learn that the Don Cossack list received 640,000 votes (45 percent of the total) (V. A. Antonov-Ovseenko, *Zapiski o grazhdanskoi voine*, I [Moscow, 1924], 194). It is apparent that this is approximately the correct figure, and that statements fixing the vote at 900,000 or above are gross exaggerations (see, for example, K. P. Kakliugin, "Voiskovoi Ataman A. M. Kaledin i ego vremia," *Donskaia Letopis*, no. 2 [1923], p. 124).

[9] "Narodnicheskii sotsializm — gnilaia i smerdiashchaia mertvechina" (Narodnik socialism is foul and stinking carrion), wrote Lenin on one occasion ("Chto delaetsia v narodnichestve i chto delaetsia v derevne?" *Sochineniia* (2nd ed.), XVI [1912–13], 312).

in Western lands under the influence of the Roman law.[10] Whether they would have developed a property consciousness once they were in actual possession of the land is, of course, a moot question, but one of sufficient validity to cause the impartial observer to view with skepticism the exultations of Narodnik spokesmen who hailed the election as a grandiose triumph for collectivism.[11]

But if the victory of socialism was inconclusive, what can be said about the showing on the other side, where the adherents of the traditional order of society were gathered under the banner of the Constitutional Democrats and in a number of special interest groups? These people had sustained a dreadful beating at the polls; they had experienced not so much a walloping as a washout. They were not even in the running, for the main fight had taken place within the revolutionary camp, between the Bolshevik wing of the Social Democrats and the SR branch of the Populist movement. It is true that to the figures given under the heading of Russian nonsocialist parties must be added a considerable number of Cossack votes from Orenburg and eastern Siberia, which appear in the residue of 2,151,368 votes in the third column but which are not indicated separately in the sources and hence can only roughly be estimated.[12] Even complete returns from the Cossack districts,

---

[10] In Russia the principles of the Roman law were too recently established and too restricted in scope to have acquired dominion over the minds of the people. This had been one of the points of departure for the Socialist Revolutionaries in constructing their ideology. See *Protokoly pervago sezda partii sotsialistov-revoliutsionerov* (n.p., 1906), pp. 207, 220–228; "Agrarnaia programma russkoi sotsial-demokratii," *Revoliutsionnaia Rossiia*, no. 40 (January 15, 1904), p. 9; and especially V. M. Chernov, *Zemlia i pravo: Sbornik statei* (Petrograd, 1919), pp. 130–131, 133–134, 167.

[11] So Sviatitski, *Kogo russkii narod izbral svoimi predstaviteliami?*, p. 7, and "Itogi vyborov," *God russkoi revoliutsii*, p. 119.

[12] In Orenburg the SR's got two seats with 110,172 votes and the Bolsheviks three with 163,425; therefore the Orenburg Cossack list must have received in excess of 200,000 votes, since four seats were obtained. Here the residue of 378,511 was swelled by the Bashkir Federalists, who won two places (base figures from AOR, *Vserossiiskoe Uchreditelnoe Sobranie*, p. xxviii; Cossack seats ascertained from list of members of the Constituent Assembly, in *ibid.*, pp. 116–138). Sviatitski assigns 56,050 votes to the Cossacks in eastern Siberia on the basis of partial returns (*Itogi vyborov*, p. 36). As this is a lump sum, undivided by districts, it is necessarily placed in the residue.

THE VOTE BY PARTIES FOR THE WHOLE COUNTRY

	Sviatitski	AOR	Present Study
RUSSIAN SOCIALIST PARTIES			
SR	16,509,756[a]	17,490,837[b]	15,848,004
SD Bolshevik	9,023,963	9,562,358	9,844,637
SD Menshevik	668,064	1,248,958	1,364,826
Popular Socialist	312,038	?	322,078[c]
Other socialist	211,187	?	183,512
RUSSIAN NONSOCIALIST PARTIES			
Const. Democratic	1,856,639	?	1,986,601
Cossack	79,162	?	663,112
Landowner	215,542	?	171,245
Right	292,133	?	109,161
Orthodox		?	155,341
Old Believer	73,464	?	53,999
Other Christian	....	?	18,179
Other nonsocialist	....	?	91,381
UKRAINIAN PARTIES			
Ukr. Socialist Bloc	506,887	?	3,556,581
Ukr. SR	3,433,574[d]	3,433,574[d]	1,286,157
Ukr. SD	95,117	?	95,117
Minor groups	....	?	19,212
Total	4,035,578		4,957,067
Joint lists:			
Ukr. SR and SR[e]	....	?	1,203,135
Ukr. SR and Left SR ..	....	?	11,871
Ukr. SR, Ukr. SD, and Jewish Socialist	....	?	4,219
Ukr. and Tatar	....	?	53,000
Total	....		1,272,225
MOHAMMEDAN PARTIES			
Mohammedan Nationalist .	576,693	?	484,464
Mohammedan Left and SR	515,272	?	458,272
Total	1,091,965		942,736
OTHER NATIONALITIES			
Armenian Dashnaktsutiun .	....	?	over 350,000
Bashkir	195,230	?	13,100
Buriat	65,403	?	15,464

Chuvash	235,547	?	235,552
Esthonian:			
Nonsocialist	....	?	85,107
Labor	....	?	64,704
SR	....	?	17,726
SD	....	?	9,244
Total	....		176,781
Finnish Socialist	14,000	?	....
German:			
Nationalist	130,579	?	121,614
Socialist	44,507	?	42,156
Total	175,086		163,770
Greek	.....	..	9,143
Jewish:			
Nationalist, etc.	550,075	?	417,215
Bund	....	?	31,123
Poalei Zion	....	?	20,538
Other socialist	....	?	29,322
Total	....		498,198
Lettish	67,508	?	69,242
Polish	154,809	?	125,240
White Russian	12,007	?	15,517
Other national	....	?	6,224
Total	....		1,678,231
Nonclassified residue	417,804	?	2,151,368[f]
TOTALS FOR COUNTRY	36,256,960	not given	41,686,876[g]

[a] Includes 1,228,535 votes cast jointly for SR's and Ukrainian SR's and hence inseparable; includes also 1,020,000 votes arbitrarily assigned to Mogilev and the Caucasian Front. Observance of same standards of accuracy as in the third column would cut total without more ado to 14,261,221.

[b] Includes same inaccuracies as above except in case of Mogilev province, for which actual returns were available. This is apparent from study of AOR: *Vserossiiskoe Uchreditelnoe Sobranie*, p. xxviii and p. 210, n. 13.

[c] Includes several joint lists with kindred groups.

[d] Includes civilian districts (e.g., Kiev) where joint list with Ukrainian SD's was presented. Hence inaccurate, though most votes cast for the Ukrainian socialist bloc were undoubtedly SR rather than SD.

[e] Included by Sviatitski in SR total, but inseparable and can not be assigned to either group. See note *a* above.

[f] Includes all votes known to have been cast but not identifiable by party. Of this total 1,167,974 are contributed by the Soviet source. See note 8 in this chapter.

[g] Eliminating duplication of 126,827 votes in Olonets province where special electoral system prevailed. Here there were two seats to be filled and only two candidates, one SR and one Menshevik, each voter having two votes.

however, would not raise the total conservative vote above 3,500,000 out of a grand total of nearly 42,000,000.

These figures tell us a great deal. They reveal in stark outline certain of the fundamental weaknesses of Old Russia: the numerical insignificance of the middle class, the loss of vitality of once powerful institutions like the monarchy and the church, and the absence of a strong national consciousness such as had come to the rescue of Western conservatism when the old mainstays of monarchism and clericalism began to give way. One can only marvel at the eclipse of clerical influence, at the miserable showing not only of the Orthodox candidates but also of the Old Believers, who between them could not muster a quarter of a million followers at the polls. Except in the Mohammedan communities of the east, the priesthood had ceased to be an important political factor. The support of the extreme right overlapped that of the clergy but was equally ineffective; only in Nizhni Novgorod province did their combined forces make a real showing.[13] It seems ironical that the landowners' ticket, the prospects of which could not conceivably have been darker than in November of 1917, should have drawn more votes on the conservative side than any other save only the Kadet and the Cossack.

The weakness of Great Russian nationalism contrasts markedly with the spirit of lesser ethnic groups, now released from the restraints imposed by tsarism and asserting their separate identity — often, it would seem, with more vigor than validity. The five million votes obtained in the clear by the various Ukrainian lists constitute an impressive showing from any point of view, and must be augmented by at least another half million votes as the Ukrainian share of the joint lists agreed on with other parties. However one may estimate the strength of Ukrainian separatism,

[13] The list headed by Archbishop Sergius received 48,428 votes out of a total of 579,897. One source speaks of it as the Faith and Fatherland list; another, as the Christian Union (*Izvestiia Vserossiiskoi po delam o vyborakh v Uchreditelnoe Sobranie Komissii*, no. 24 [December 16, 1917], p. 4; AOR, *Vserossiiskoe Uchreditelnoe Sobranie*, p. 137). In column 3 it appears under Orthodox.

no one can deny that Little Russian particularism had real force behind it. The reverse is true in White Russia, where it is scarcely possible to speak of a particularistic consciousness in the light of the wholly negligible quantity of votes cast for White Russian lists in Vitebsk and Minsk provinces and on the Western Front.

About a million votes had gone to Mohammedan lists, either to those regarded as leftist because of a tinge of Narodnik socialism, or to those ranked as conservative because of a nationalist label. This convincing demonstration of strength in itself becomes still more impressive when the origin of the votes is considered, for nearly all of them were amassed along the Volga or in the Ural region, without reference to the great Mohammedan stronghold of Central Asia, where no election was held,[14] or to the Transcaucasus, for which no separate returns are available.[15] Since in the Urals and along the Volga the Mohammedan confession and Tatar nationality are virtually synonymous, and since here the Tatars have been engulfed by the tide of Russian expansion and their identity endangered, it is proper to regard this vote as more a tribute to Tatar nationalism than to the Prophet's cult. List designations, in fact, bear this out with headings such as "Musulman National Council" or "Musulman National Committee." As conclusive proof, it may be pointed out that the Bashkirs, who

[14] Such, at any rate, is the commonly accepted version. See Vishniak, *Vserossiiskoe Uchreditelnoe Sobranie*, pp. 91–92. Sviatitski's table contains no returns from Central Asia. However, in another article he lists an SR member from the Fergana district of Turkestan. See "Fraktsiia partii S.-R. Uchreditelnago Sobraniia i eia deiatelnost," *Partiinyia Izvestiia*, no. 5 (Jan. 20, 1918), pp. 32–36. A strange contradiction is to be noted in the Soviet study: in the foreword to the list of members of the Constituent Assembly the editors state that there were none from Fergana (AOR, *Vserossiiskoe Uchreditelnoe Sobranie*, p. 115), and then in the list itself they proceed to give no less than five delegates from Fergana, including the one mentioned by Sviatitski (*ibid.*, pp. 134, 137, 138).

[15] The Mohammedan vote in the Transcaucasus is lumped with many others in the general residue of 2,151,368. Though the vote itself cannot be ascertained, the deputies returned can be picked out from the general list. There were twelve of them, of whom seven were elected on the main list, the Musulman National Committee and the Musavat party (*ibid.*, pp. 116*ff*). Since the Mensheviks in the Transcaucasus secured 14 seats with 569,362 votes, the total Mohammedan vote must have been about half a million.

likewise are Mohammedans, ran their own candidates on separate lists in competition with their Tatar co-religionists.[16]

Of the non-Moslem ethnic groups in the east of Russia only the Chuvash, with their quarter of a million votes, made any considerable showing. Finnish tribes like the Mordvins and Cheremis were either too inert or too nearly assimilated to seek political expression apart from the main Russian parties.[17]

In general it can be said that the provinces on the periphery of Russia, northwest, west, south, and east, yielded a very large contingent of votes for the national minorities. In many-peopled Transcaucasia there was an impressive turnout in the case of the Armenians, whose revolutionary organization, the Dashnaktsutiun, secured ten seats in the Constituent Assembly.[18] Where German or Polish elements formed a substantial part of the population, their own national lists were favored. The Jews, as might be expected, proved to be a highly articulate group, with many of their voters preferring some specifically Jewish list to those of the big supernational parties. The Lettish and Esthonian vote, though considerable, was much less than it could have been, partly because of the German occupation of Courland and Riga, but mainly because of the great strength displayed in the Baltic provinces by the local SD affiliate of Bolshevism.

In respect to the apportionment of seats in the Constituent Assembly, the Archives of the October Revolution have painstakingly assembled a list of 707 deputies, divided into the following partisan groupings: [19]

---

[16] Bashkir lists were offered in Samara, Perm, Ufa, and Orenburg provinces. Two deputies were elected from Orenburg, two from Ufa, and one from Perm (*ibid.*). Sviatitski credits the Bashkirs with 195,230 votes ("Itogi vyborov," *God russkoi revoliutsii*, p. 119), but he had no returns from Orenburg. This writer does not have the figures by districts save for Samara, where the vote was negligible (13,100).

[17] In Viatka the Cheremis did have a joint list with the Popular Socialists.

[18] As singled out from the list of members in AOR, *Vserossiiskoe Uchreditelnoe Sobranie*, pp. 116*ff.* The figure of 350,000, taken from the *Delo Naroda*, no. 228 (December 9, 1917), and given in the table above, constituted the bulk of the Armenian vote but apparently was still not definitive.

[19] AOR, *Vserossiiskoe Uchreditelnoe Sobranie*, p. 115. The editors concede that on the basis of existing records it is not possible to determine with

SR's	370
Left SR's[20]	40
Bolsheviks	175
Mensheviks	16
Popular Socialists	2
Kadets	17
National groups	86
Unknown	1

A more detailed classification is given by Sviatitski on the basis of virtually the same number of deputies, elected as of the middle of January 1918.[21] For purposes of comparison, the same combinations are indicated in the second column as are employed in the foregoing tabulation.

SR's proper	299 }	380
Ukrainian SR's[22]	81 }	
Left SR's	39	
Bolsheviks	168	
Mensheviks	18	
Popular Socialists	4	
Constitutional Democrats ...	15 }	17
Rightists	2 }	
Musulmans, Bashkirs, Kirghiz	28 ⎤	
Armenians	10	
Jews, Poles, Letts, Esthonians	9	
National SR groups[23]	19	77
Ukrainian SD's	2	
Cossacks	9 ⎦	
Total	703	

---

exactitude the party affiliation of the deputies; they claim only to have made a fair approximation in submitting these figures. The editors were much more concerned with compiling the list of members (pp. 116–138) than with compiling the numerical results and consequently did a much better job.

[20] Schism in PSR developed after election was held. See p. 72.

[21] *Kogo russkii narod izbral svoimi predstaviteliami?*, pp. 10–11. The author places the total number of seats to be filled at 817. The Soviet study (p. 115) mentions 815; the number of seats allotted to each civilian district is given in the table, pp. 140–142. The hundred-odd deputies who do not figure in the above tabulations were never chosen. See above, pp. 6, 19.

[22] The Soviet study (p. 213, n. 21) mentions 69 Ukrainian SR's as elected in nine civilian districts. The number elected at the front is not given.

[23] Musulman, Chuvash, Moldavian, and Buriat.

It is not possible to go beyond these tabulations, as they contain the full complement of deputies elected in districts for which neither Sviatitski nor the Archives of the October Revolution could produce the actual returns (for example, Kaluga, Bessarabia, Podolia, Olonets, Baltic Fleet, Esthonia). They may be considered, therefore, as substantially complete.

CHAPTER III

ANALYSIS OF RETURNS FOR REPRESENTATIVE DISTRICTS

So MUCH for a general survey of the results of the election, based on the country-wide totals for each party. In so vast and varied a land as Russia, however, it is necessary to do more than present a general survey, and not so much for the sake of completeness as for clarity and comprehension. Only a more detailed inspection can reveal significant features of the election, for Russia is no compact nation-state but rather a spacious empire, in which factors of class, location, and nationality are all involved in varying proportions. Country-wide totals, therefore, are not simply a projection of more or less uniform local results but rather a composite of regional returns which often are sharply at variance with one another. Nor is this difference induced solely by diversity of race and religion; the behavior of the same class of the same nationality may vary from region to region, as was notably true of the Great Russian peasantry in the central region around Moscow and in the black-earth zone to the south and southeast. In these two regions difference in soil gave rise to a different economic setup, and this in turn united with other factors to produce a different political outlook.

A number of electoral districts, therefore, have been singled out for closer inspection and analysis, each being representative of a certain region and free from defects in the statistical sense. Let us begin with the northwestern or lake region and proceed through Great Russia in an easterly and southeasterly direction, reserving other portions of the empire for later analysis.

Among the four provinces in the lake region, Novgorod is the most suitable. The election results there are given in the accompanying table.[1]

[1] *Delo Naroda*, no. 228 (December 9, 1917); *Pravda*, no. 205 (December 3, 1917). Figures are unofficial.

Lake or Northwestern Region: Novgorod Province

SR	220,665
Bolshevik	203,658
Kadet	31,480
Menshevik	9,336
Popular Socialist	10,314
Landowner	7,804
House-owner	1,178
Coöperative	1,123
Unity (Plekhanov)	860
Total	486,418

Here the contest lay between the Socialist Revolutionaries and the Bolsheviks, the Kadets trailing far behind. Novgorod was not an industrial province; how, then, could a Marxist party fare so well in a rural constituency? The answer is to be found in the close economic ties between the Novgorod peasantry and the working class of St. Petersburg, whither many inhabitants of other provinces — and particularly of Novgorod — [2] were accustomed to repair in search of seasonal employment without, however, surrendering their peasant status at home. This half-proletarian, half-peasant type was a common phenomenon in northern Russia, and its prevalence goes far to explain why, in 1917, Bolshevism should have spread with such rapidity from industrial centers into the surrounding countryside. If the peasant did not have a share in industry himself, he was likely to have family connections with the proletariat, itself still raw and green, and but one step removed from the soil.

The influence of the town on the country is still more pronounced in the central industrial region, where peasants were drawn not only to both metropolises but also to the lesser industrial centers of their own provinces. Vladimir, with its many textile mills at Ivanovo-Voznesensk and elsewhere, was the most extensively industrialized province in the region, aside from Mos-

[2] *Rossiia: Polnoe geograficheskoe opisanie nashego otechestva*, ed. V. P. Semenov (St. Petersburg: A. F. Devrien, 1899–1914), Vol. III, *Ozernaia Oblast*, p. 206.

cow itself. Here Bolshevism had always commanded a following, and by the fall of 1917 virtually the entire proletariat had rallied to Lenin's standard, turning its back on Menshevism and pulling a large part of the peasantry away from the Socialist Revolutionaries. As a consequence, the Bolsheviks achieved an absolute majority in the balloting for the Constituent Assembly, as shown in the accompanying tabulation.[3]

Central Industrial Region: Vladimir Province

SR	197,311
Bolshevik	337,941
Kadet	38,035
Menshevik	13,074
Popular Socialist	6,908
Coöperative	1,482
Right ("Regeneration")	9,209
Total	603,960

Again, we have a duel between two parties. But this time the tables are turned, for in Vladimir there is a numerous and strong-willed proletariat, as there was not in Novgorod, and many of the peasants are drawn along in its wake. Of the thirteen *uezds* into which the province was divided, only two were carried by the SR's, and these were precisely the most remote and the least developed industrially.[4] Rarely can so perfect a correlation between political, geographical, and economic factors be found. The Constitutional Democrats are no stronger here than in Novgorod, polling only 6.3 per cent of the total vote; the Mensheviks fare very badly;

[3] N. Shakhanov, *1917-yi god vo Vladimirskoi gubernii: Khronika sobytii* (Vladimir, 1927), pp. 128–130, 139, quoting from the local press. Figures are complete but unofficial. Other sources (including Sviatitski) differ slightly, but are based on earlier returns and hence are rejected.

[4] They gained a plurality (42.4 per cent) in Viazniki *uezd*, which lay to the east of the industrial belt but had some linen and hemp weaving, and won decisively (57.4 per cent of the vote) in Gorokhovets *uezd*, situated still further to the east and containing no factories whatever (according to the census of 1897) (*Rossiia: Polnoe geograficheskoe opisanie*, Vol. I, *Moskovskaia promyshlennaia oblast i Verkhnee Povolzhe*, pp. 86, 312–313; electoral figures from Shakhanov).

there are some Popular Socialists in Vladimir as in Novgorod, but not many; the members of the coöperative societies, and even their employees, obviously do not share the desire of a few high functionaries like Berkenheim to bring the movement into politics; [5] a group of reactionaries comes out into the open and bids for support, but elicits only a weak response from the electorate (1.5 per cent of the whole).

These results in what for Russia was a highly industrialized district stand in glaring contrast to those in a typical black-earth province like Kursk.[6]

Black-Earth Region: Kursk Province

SR	868,743
Bolshevik	119,127
Kadet	47,199
Menshevik	6,037
Popular Socialist	8,594
Landowner	8,656
Total	1,058,356

In Kursk there was little besides farming, and peasants were really peasants. The influence of the metropolitan centers was weak. As a consequence, the SR vote shoots upward and the Bolshevik vote drops precipitously, the ratio being better than 7:1. Even so, Lenin's party still occupies second place with more than 100,000 votes, relatively few of which could be proletarian. How, then, were they obtained? The answer is that soldiers — either those from rear garrisons or those coming back from the front — everywhere conducted a fierce agitation on behalf of Bolshevism and disposed numbers of peasants in favor of a party which otherwise they almost certainly would have passed up.[7] Thus was Bolshe-

[5] Sviatitski, as a good SR, celebrates the fiasco of the coöperatives at the polls, since their political venture could have succeeded only at the cost of his party ("Itogi vyborov," *God russkoi revoliutsii*, p. 118).

[6] *Izvestiia Vserossiiskoi po delam o vyborakh v Uchreditelnoe Sobranie Komissii*, no. 24 (December 16, 1917), p. 3. Returns are complete and official — a rare occurrence.

[7] This phenomenon will be discussed in Chapters IV and V.

vism sustained in districts with little or no industry. The Kadets are as weak here as elsewhere, the Mensheviks even weaker, while the Popular Socialists continue steady in their insignificance. The right is represented in Kursk by a landowners' list, which gets the votes of . . . landowners. One notes the simplicity of the electoral pattern in Kursk — despite the presence of a large Little Russian element [8] in the southern *uezds*, it is a remarkably homogeneous province in every sense of the word.

The same cannot be said of the provinces in the Kama-Ural region, the next that claims our attention. Ethnographical diversity is reflected in a more complex table than hitherto.[9]

Kama-Ural Region: Kazañ Province

SR	260,000
Bolshevik	50,000
Kadet	32,000
Menshevik	4,906
Coöperative and Independent Socialist	2,993
Orthodox	12,000
Bourgeois splinter	2,000
Right SR's	10,000
Mohammedan Socialists	153,151
Mohammedan Nationalists	100,000
Chuvash	226,496
Residue	5,050
Total	858,596

There is a large Chuvash vote — claimed by the SR's [10] — and a

[8] 580,000 by the census of 1897. The Little Russians, however, had not retained their purity of type and had mixed to a considerable extent with their Great Russian neighbors (*Rossiia: Polnoe geograficheskoe opisanie*, Vol. II, *Srednerusskaia chernozëmnaia oblast*, pp. 168–169).

[9] *Russkiia Vedomosti*, no. 277 (December 29, 1917). The round numbers, of course, indicate approximate figures only. For a number of reasons it would have been better to take Perm or Ufa instead of Kazañ, but no returns are available except those in Sviatitski, and he does not give a complete breakdown by parties.

[10] Sviatitski, "Itogi vyborov," *God russkoi revoliutsii*, p. 112, and *Kogo russkii narod izbral svoimi predstaviteliami?*, p. 4. But the list was a com-

large Tatar (Mohammedan) vote, divided between left and right in the ratio of 3:2. The bulk of the Russian population again prefers the PSR, while the Kadets and Mensheviks betray their customary weakness. But Bolshevism, also, is weak in Kazañ — a surprising circumstance in view of the outstanding military significance of the city and district and the fact that Kazañ was the station of one of the largest interior garrisons in the country.[11] The explanation probably lies both in the presence of a large native element, much less responsive to Bolshevik propaganda than the Russians themselves, and in the special conditions within the SR organization, which in Kazañ province had fallen under the domination of its left wing, the violent and semi-anarchistic preachings of which afforded a thoroughly radical alternative to Bolshevism. Hence the local schism in the PSR and the attempt of the right wing to run its own ticket, which ended in fiasco.[12] The 12,000 votes cast under the banner of Orthodoxy show that the political influence of the clergy was as little marked here as elsewhere, despite the presence of a rival faith, which presumably should have sharpened religious loyalties.

Proceeding now across the Urals into western Siberia, we encounter once more, as in the case of the black-earth zone, an electoral pattern that is simple and clear: [13]

---

posite one and was designated as that of the "General Chuvash National Congress, Chuvash Military Committee, and Chuvash PSR." See under Gavriil F. Aliunov, deputy from Kazañ, in the list of members of the Constituent Assembly, AOR, *Vserossiiskoe Uchreditelnoe Sobranie*, p. 116.

[11] N. Ezhov, *Voennaia Kazañ v 1917g. Kratkii otchet* (Kazañ, 1927), pp. 6–8. Soldiers everywhere were notoriously susceptible to Bolshevik blandishments. The Kazañ military district embraced a vast territory (10 provinces and 2 regions), the administration of which centered in the city.

[12] In general the SR voters went for the label without bothering to find out whether it covered a leftist or centrist or rightist selection of candidates. It all depended on which faction controlled the provincial organization and drew up the list. Dissident tickets, whether of the left or right, were regularly voted down.

[13] Sviatitsky, *Itogi vyborov*, pp. 34–36. Sviatitski ascribes to Tomsk 8,048 votes cast for a German list, but it is clear from his own figures that these votes should have been included in the returns from the Altai district instead of from Tomsk.

Siberia: Tomsk Province

SR	541,153
Bolshevik	51,456
Kadet	18,618
Menshevik	5,769
Popular Socialist	15,802
Coöperative	2,686
Total	635,484

Here in territory where neither the influence of the large cities nor of the front was felt at first-hand, the SR's had swept the field, polling 85 per cent of the vote and increasing the ratio between themselves and the second-place Bolsheviks even beyond what it had been for the black-earth province of Kursk. The other parties hardly figure at all: the Popular Socialists, though stronger here than elsewhere, still fall wide of electing a single deputy. In eastern Siberia, with its mining districts and substantial labor movement, the Bolsheviks did somewhat better and the SR victory was less one-sided,[14] but the population here was thinner, so that, taken as a whole, Siberia gave the SR's a larger percentage of votes than any other region.[15]

Turning from a survey of the regions of Great Russia to Little Russia, we encounter the most complex electoral pattern of any yet examined. The most purely Ukrainian of all parts of the Ukraine is Poltava province,[16] and, as fate would have it, the election returns from there are complete and official — a welcome exception to the rule. They afford, therefore, an excellent insight into the distribution of strength in the Ukraine: [17]

[14] In the Ienisei district, for example, the SR's received 229,671 votes against 96,138 for the Bolsheviks (*Izvestiia Vserossiiskoi po delam o vyborakh v Uchreditelnoe Sobranie Komissii*, no. 24 [December 16, 1917], p. 3).

[15] Lenin, "Vybory v Uchreditelnoe Sobranie i diktatura proletariata," *Sochineniia* (2nd ed.), XXIV, 632, where the figure is given as 75 per cent, based on the statistics of Sviatitski.

[16] 97.6 per cent of the population was Little Russian in 1897 (*Rossiia: Polnoe geograficheskoe opisanie*, Vol. VII, *Malorossiia*, p. 98).

[17] *Izvestiia Vserossiiskoi po delam o vyborakh v Uchreditelnoe Sobranie Komissii*, no. 24 (December 16, 1917), pp. 4, 7.

Little Russia: Poltava Province

SR and Ukrainian SR (joint list)	198,437
Bolshevik	64,460
Kadet	18,105
Menshevik and Jewish Bund	5,993
Popular Socialist and Coöperatives	4,391
Landowner	61,115
Ukrainian SR	727,247
Ukrainian SD	22,613
Ukrainian Socialist Federalist	9,092
Ukrainian National Republican	1,070
Jewish National Committee	13,722
Jewish list	12,100
Jewish People's Party	6,448
Jewish Socialist Workers' Party	1,482
Poalei Zion	879
Local peasants' soviet	445
List without title	1,657
Total	1,149,256

No other district presents more interesting or more revealing figures. The one thing that stands out most clearly is the strength of Ukrainian sentiment. The voters in Poltava province were confronted with two lists — one offered by the Ukrainian SR's standing alone, the other in combination with the All-Russian SR party, here dominated by its left wing and hence prepared to go the limit in meeting autonomist demands. Either list would have afforded an outlet to nationalist sentiment, yet the voters chose the simon-pure Ukrainian SR list in the ratio of 7:2. In the face of such a clear-cut demonstration of strength, it is simply not possible to contend that the Ukrainian movement was a weak and artificial thing, concocted by a group of hyper-nationalistic intellectuals; yet it would also be inadmissible to contend that the returns indicate a desire for separation from Russia. If the assertion of the Great Russian chauvinists is definitely disproved, the claim of the Little Russian separatists is not substantiated. What happened was that the Little Russian peasantry followed the lead of the intellectuals in an impressive manifestation of devotion to their folkways without by any means implying that they desired the independent statehood toward which the intellectuals were steadily gravitating. There is no reason to assume that the peasant voters would not have been satisfied with autonomy within the framework of a federal state, even though the intellectuals who led them might not have been. Little Russian particularism is not necessarily identical with Ukrainian separatism.

In keeping with the almost exclusively agrarian character of the Ukrainian people, it will be noted that the other Ukrainian parties polled scarcely any votes at all, the Ukrainian SD's having less than one-thirtieth the strength of their agrarian rivals. The parties of All-Russian significance attracted little strength in Poltava province: Bolshevism was weak here, but not nearly so weak as Menshevism; among the conservative groups, the Kadets with their Great Russian bias were quite outdistanced in this opulent farming region by the landowners' list, which did better here than anywhere else in the country.[18]

Quite different is the picture in White Russia, where Vitebsk province may be taken as indicative of the general trend.[19] Two

White Russia: Vitebsk Province

SR	150,279
Bolshevik	287,101
Kadet	8,132
Menshevik and Bund	12,471
Popular Socialist	3,599
Landowner	6,098
Peasants' list	9,752
White Russian	9,019
Lettish Socialist Federalist	26,990
Lettish Nationalist	5,881
Letgallian Nationalist	5,118
Jewish Nationalist	24,790
Polish Nationalist	10,556
Splinter	752
Total	560,538

[18] Regarding the nature of this party in the Ukraine, see Chapter IV, note 18.

[19] *Delo Naroda*, no. 220 (November 30, 1917). This source gives the total as 560,540.

features stand out from these returns: the weakness of White
Russian particularism and the strength of Bolshevism. Whether
because there was less to build on or because the intellectuals were
slower in getting started, the White Russian movement was only
a tiny trickle compared to the broad stream of Ukrainian nationalism, and was quite overshadowed in voting strength by the
minority groups of Letts, Poles, and Jews. Aside from these, the
population had been content to divide its suffrage among the parties of All-Russian significance, and almost exclusively between
the Bolsheviks and the SR's, the former having decidedly the
upper hand in this province. There is no satisfactory explanation
of the fact that the Bolsheviks inflicted a stinging defeat on the
SR's in two White Russian provinces — Vitebsk and Minsk [20] —
only themselves to sustain a rout in a third province, Mogilev.[21]
The influence of the front with its milling mob of Bolshevized
soldiers was no doubt of great moment in Vitebsk and Minsk,[22]
but such influence must also have extended to Mogilev province —
after all, general headquarters was at Mogilev on the Dnieper.[23]
The provinces of Vitebsk and Minsk resemble those of the central
industrial region in that only in these parts of the country did

[20] In Vitebsk province, the SR vote was 27 per cent of the total (see table
above); in Minsk province, 20 per cent of the total (computed from figures
in *Izvestiia Vserossiiskoi po delam o vyborakh v Uchreditelnoe Sobranie
Komissii*, no. 24 [December 16, 1917], pp. 3–4).

[21] As previously stated, no valid returns have ever been published for
this district. But the SR vote was 70 per cent of the total (AOR, *Vserossiiskoe Uchreditelnoe Sobranie*, p. 210, n. 13). Twelve SR's were elected from
Mogilev province, as against only one Bolshevik and two Jewish deputies.
See report in Sviatitski, "Fraktsiia partii S.-R. Uchreditelnago Sobraniia i
eia deiatelnost," *Partiinyia Izvestiia*, no. 5, pp. 32–36.

[22] *Novaia Zhizn*, no. 201 (December 14, 1917); V. Knorin, *Revoliutsiia i
kontr-revoliutsiia v Belorussii (fevral 1917–fevral 1918)*, Part I (Smolensk,
1920), pp. 58, 61, 63. The Minsk correspondent of Gorki's paper states that
war weariness was at its maximum close to the front. Minsk was closer than
Mogilev, it is true, but the difference in proximity would hardly account for
the phenomenon in question.

[23] Of possible influence on the election was the very great popularity
enjoyed by the SR head of the Mogilev provincial soviet of peasants'
deputies. See N. Ia. Bykhovski, *Vserossiiskii sovet krestianskikh deputatov
1917g.* (Moscow, 1929), p. 170.

the peasantry favor the Bolsheviks over the SR's. One difference, however, was that the Kadet party, weak everywhere, virtually did not exist in White Russia.

For the non-Russian portions of the empire there are satisfactory returns only in the case of the Baltic Provinces, and even there one province — Courland — was eliminated by German conquest and another — Livonia — was partially occupied. The choice is thus narrowed to Esthonia, the returns for which are presented in the accompanying table.[24]

Baltic Provinces: Esthonia

SR	3,200
Bolshevik	119,863
Esthonian SR	17,726
Esthonian SD	9,244
Esthonian Laborite	64,704
Esthonian Democratic	68,085
Esthonian Land Union	17,022
Total	299,844

The field is divided between Bolshevism and Esthonian nationalism, expressed in groupings of varied economic appeal. In this land of Western culture and highly developed social forms there flourished a powerful labor movement, deep red in hue and recruited from workers on large estates as well as from factory hands.[25] The movement was closely connected with Lenin's party through a common bond of internationalism, the weakness of which in the case of other Russian parties had kept them from gaining a foothold in the Baltic Provinces. In Livonia the strength of Bolshevism was truly formidable,[26] greater than anywhere else

[24] *Pravda*, no. 206 (December 5, 1917).

[25] A great proportion of the land was in the form of estates, and the estates were individually of unusual size, much above the average for the empire as a whole.

[26] 97,781 votes of a total of 136,080, or 72 per cent, were cast for the SD's of Latvia, the Baltic affiliate of Bolshevism (*Izvestiia Vserossiiskoi po delam o vyborakh v Uchreditelnoe Sobranie Komissii*, no. 24 [December 16, 1917], p. 1).

in the empire, and the support came from the farm hands rather than the city workers, as is seen from the fact that Riga had been taken by the Germans in September and so had been removed from the scope of the election.[27]

There remain two special types of voting districts, the urban and the military. The great metropolitan centers of European Russia — there were only two in this peasant empire — had been constituted as districts in their own right, so that their political complexion is readily apparent from the returns presented in the accompanying table.[28]

	Petrograd City	*Moscow City*
SR	152,230	62,260
Bolshevik	424,027	366,148
Constitutional Democrat	246,506	263,859
Menshevik [29]	29,167	21,597
Popular Socialist	19,109	2,508
Democratic Socialist Bloc	....	35,305
Plekhanov Unity	1,823	....
Orthodox	24,139	....
Roman Catholic	14,382	....
Other religious	3,797	....
Cossack	6,712	....
Residue [30]	15,809	13,086
Total	942,333	764,763

Here the duel of the extremities is the oustanding feature of the election. Here alone in all of Russia did the Constitutional

[27] In the Vollmar district the Bolshevik vote in the town was not only absolutely but also proportionately less than in the surrounding countryside — 73 per cent in the town as against 77 per cent in the *uezd* (*Izvestiia Tsentralnago Ispolnitelnago Komiteta i petrogradskago soveta rabochikh i soldatskikh deputatov*, no. 232 [November 22, 1917], p. 7).

[28] Returns for Petrograd in *Delo Naroda*, no. 211 (November 16, 1917), revised in no. 212 (November 17, 1917); returns for Moscow in *Russkiia Vedomosti*, no. 257 (November 24, 1917).

[29] Schism resulted in two lists in each city: SD (United) and SD (Internationalist). Combined vote given here.

[30] Includes 5,310 votes for a feminist list and 4,696 for the right SR's in the case of Petrograd; includes 4,085 votes for a non-partisan list (probably rightist) in Moscow.

Democrats make a real showing. The election reveals, paradoxically, that the great strongholds of Bolshevism were also the strongholds of the class enemy, for the proletariat was complemented by a numerous bourgeoisie in these centers of business life, and the bourgeoisie was reinforced by government functionaries who staffed the bureaus of the capital and the second administrative center of the empire. These civil servants were rabid against the Bolsheviks, regarding them as enemies of the Russian state. Political consciousness was more highly developed in the big cities than elsewhere and class lines more tightly drawn, the social cleavage being especially marked in the case of Moscow, ⁻here almost nothing had been left in between to mitigate the lash of extremes. The SR organization in Petrograd, controlled ince September by the left wing of the party,[31] still retained a considerable portion of the following which had made it the strongest party in the capital as recently as the preceding August,[32] but in Moscow the organization had gone to pieces and its support had drained off in two directions, much of it going to the Kadets but more to the Bolsheviks.[33] Finally, it will be noted that in Petrograd the attempt of the extreme right to rally support under a religious banner had ended in failure; virtually the entire nonsocialist electorate, regardless of political shading, had given its suffrage to the Constitutional Democratic party, among whose adherents on this occasion there were no doubt many who were neither constitutionalists nor democrats.[34]

The great, swollen army of Russia, with its millions of reluctant soldiers, had been granted the suffrage. To have withheld it would have meant attainting the election, so large was the segment of population that had been drawn into the war. Each of the five main fronts had been constituted an electoral district, and two more were provided for the sailors, one for the Baltic and one

[31] Control had been wrested from the hands of the centrist faction at the VII city conference (*Delo Naroda*, no. 152, September 12, 1917).

[32] As demonstrated by the municipal election of August 20.

[33] There had been a catastrophic falling off in the SR vote, from 374,885 in the municipal election in June to 62,260 in November. See pp. 52–53.

[34] See Chapter VI, note 9.

for the Black Sea Fleet. The voting at the front and in the navy seems to have been determined by one circumstance alone — the extent to which Bolshevik agitation had been carried on among the rank and file. If the district were remote from the metropolitan centers, and specifically from the influence of the Petrograd Soviet and the Bolshevik party organization, the SR's carried the day, and the farther removed the district was, the greater their degree of success; but on the Northern and Western Fronts the old-line agrarian appeal of the PSR had been overbalanced by intensive propaganda in favor of immediate peace and immediate seizure of the estates, so that here the SR's sustained a crushing defeat and Lenin's party won a great victory.[35] The contrast is seen in the accompanying tabulation.[36]

	Western Front	*Roumanian Front*
SR	180,582	679,471
Bolshevik	653,430	167,000
Constitutional Democrat	16,750	21,438
Menshevik	8,000	33,858
Ukrainian Socialist Bloc	85,062	180,576
Residue [37]	32,176	46,257
Total	976,000	1,128,600

The observer can only wonder whether the Roumanian Front would have differed from the Western had it not been more insulated against the Bolshevik contagion. Certainly the facts point in that direction. Between the two fronts lay the Southwestern,

[35] For comment of Lenin himself, see "Vybory v Uchreditelnoe Sobranie i diktatura proletariata," *Sochineniia* (2nd ed.), **XXIV**, 638.

[36] Figures are from Sviatitski's table; it has not been possible to improve on them. In the case of the Northern Front alone has the author of the present study succeeded in locating the complete and official returns. The Western and Roumanian fronts are used here because of the sharpness of the contrast involved.

[37] An earlier tabulation for the Western Front, based on a total of 544,034 votes, gave 15,113 for the Mohammedan Socialists, 3,510 for the White Russians, 3,055 for the Russian Democrats, and 2,429 for the joint Popular Socialist–Plekhanov Unity list (*Izvestiia Tsentralnago Ispolnitelnago Komiteta i petrogradskago soveta*, no. 248 [December 10, 1917], p. 4).

and here the SR's were already stronger than their rivals, though only by a ratio of 4:3. On the other hand, the Caucasian Front was even more remote than the Roumanian, and it was precisely here that the SR's displayed their greatest strength, electing five deputies against one for the Bolsheviks on the basis of incomplete returns.[38] The explanation of their success is simple: the SR leadership of the soldiers' soviets, strongly in favor of national defense, had used its authority to throttle Bolshevik agitation on the front, even denying to that party representation on electoral information committees,[39] and had gotten away with its one-sided policy because of remoteness from the hearth of revolution. Thus the strength of Bolshevism steadily wanes as the influence of the metropolitan centers recedes.[40] Not only the SR's but also the Mensheviks were helped by distance: thus on the Western Front Menshevism was already virtually extinct by the time of the election, whereas on the Roumanian Front it still retained a following, albeit a modest one. The figures presented above show that Constitutional Democracy had no appeal for the rank and file of the troops — few besides the officers could have chosen its list. On the other hand, the figures reveal that the Ukrainian movement had achieved a not inconsiderable following at the front, where leaders like Simon Petliura, deputy from the Roumanian Front, bore the standard ostensibly of Ukrainian socialism, but actually of Ukrainian nationalism.

We have now completed our survey of representative electoral

[38] Sviatitski, "Fraktsiia partii S.-R.," *Partiinyia Izvestiia*, no. 5; confirmed by a search of the list of members in AOR, *Vserossiiskoe Uchreditelnoe Sobranie*, pp. 116–138. Sviatitski gives the number of SR deputies as six in his table in the *God russkoi revoliutsii*, but this must be rejected in favor of the above. As previously stated, no returns are available for the Caucasian Front.

[39] *Revoliutsiia 1917 goda v Azerbaidzhane (khronika sobytii)*, ed. S.Belenky and A. Manvelov (Baku, 1927), pp. 124, 159; *Revoliutsiia 1917 goda v Zakavkazi (Dokumenty, Materialy)*, ed. S. E. Sef (Tiflis, 1927), pp. 84–86, 221–222, 272, 345.

[40] The same is true of the navy. The Bolsheviks overwhelmed the SR's 3 to 1 in the Baltic Fleet, only themselves to succumb by a margin of 2 to 1 in the Black Sea Fleet.

districts. Certain conclusions come readily to mind. The Bolsheviks had the center of the country — the big cities, the industrial towns, and the garrisons of the rear; they controlled those sections of the army most strategically located with reference to Moscow and Petrograd; they even commanded a strong following among the peasants of the central, White Russian, and northwestern regions. The Socialist Revolutionaries had the black-earth zone, the valley of the Volga, and Siberia; in general they were still the peasants' party, though serious defections had taken place. Particularist or separatist movements had strength in the Ukraine, along the Baltic, between the Volga and the Urals, and in the Transcaucasus; of these movements by all odds the most robust was Ukrainian nationalism. Menshevism was a spent force everywhere save in the Transcaucasus, where it was entwined with Georgian nationalism. Constitutional Democracy, for all the support that wealth and position, education and publicity could lend, had been drowned in the mass vote of peasants, soldiers, and workers. Only in Petrograd and Moscow had it marshaled real force. Even so, there was no other grouping on the conservative side that could match such little strength as the Constitutional Democrats possessed. P. N. Durnovo's prophecy had been borne out: the advocates of western constitutionalism were without roots in the Russian people.[41]

Such, broadly speaking, were the results of the election to the Constituent Assembly, expressed in terms of regional geography. They foreshadowed the distribution of strength and the territorial complexion of the approaching civil war. The deep significance of the election in this respect was not lost on Lenin, despite the

[41] "Zapiska," *Krasnaia Nov*, no. 6/10 (November–December 1922), pp. 195–197 (full text, pp. 182–199); English translation in F. A. Golder, *Documents of Russian History 1914–1917* (New York and London, 1927), pp. 3–23, pertinent passages pp. 19–22. This celebrated memorandum, unbelievably accurate in its prognostications, was laid before the Emperor Nicholas II in February 1914. Nothing is more indicative of the hopeless condition of the monarchy than its failure to turn to account the superlative talents of Durnovo and his enemy Witte, both of them advocates of a strong monarchical power.

embarrassment its outcome caused his regime. As he pointed out, "It was precisely in those regions where the percentage of Bolshevik votes in November 1917 was lowest that we observe the greatest success of counterrevolutionary movements . . . Precisely in these regions did Kolchak and Denikin hold on for months and months." And again, "The results of the election to the Constituent Assembly in November 1917 provide the background for the spectacle of civil war as it develops in the course of the next two years." [42] The Soviet government would hold the heart of the country while its enemies would be constrained to operate on the periphery — an inestimable advantage for the one and a fateful handicap for the other. The Soviet government, though badly beaten in the election, had strength where it counted most and would be able to muster enough force "in decisive spots at the decisive moment" — the words are Lenin's — to overcome its enemies and wrest from their hands the leadership of the soft-bodied Russian peasantry.[43]

[42] "Vybory v Uchreditelnoe Sobranie i diktatura proletariata," *Sochineniia* (2nd ed.), XXIV, 643, 644.

[43] This line of thought is developed in *ibid.*, pp. 634–636, 638–644.

CHAPTER IV

THE QUESTION OF VALIDITY: HOW FREE WAS THE VOTE?

THE CORRELATION between the results of the election and the lines drawn in the civil war is sufficient evidence in itself that the vote in November of 1917 was an authentic expression of the will of the Russian people. In examining the validity of an election, it is necessary to weigh two factors: the degree of fraud and intimidation and the degree of public consciousness. Was the Russian citizen reasonably free to make a choice among the contending parties, and if so, did he have any real understanding of what he was doing when he made the choice? The validity of the returns will now be examined on the basis of these two criteria, and an attempt will be made to lessen the skepticism of those who doubt that a real election could be held under the Soviet regime or that the Russian voter could stand out from the herd in the exercise of his individual judgment.

First, then, how free was the vote? There is no end of complaint in the contemporary records about intimidation of the voting public, and no absence of "incidents" at the polls or in the course of the campaign. Responsibility for such offenses is usually attributed to the Bolsheviks as people with a penchant for violence and freedom to indulge it, now that they controlled the government and had disposal of the bayonets of the garrison troops, in addition to their own private apparatus of terrorism (the Red Guard and so on). The most effective and certainly the most ubiquitous propagandists of the Bolshevik cause were the soldiers from the front and the sailors from the Baltic Fleet, men whose methods of agitation tended to be simple and direct. Trained in the violence of war, they easily resorted to that technique in dealing with the opposition; fervently desiring an end of war, they were furious at those who would not accept Lenin's formula for immediate peace.[1] Within the barracks it was often unhealthy for a soldier to betray a preference for a party other than the Bolshevik,[2] and outside the barracks the soldiers sought to intimidate the civilian population by tearing down posters of rival parties, by destroying their lists,[3] and by threatening the lives and property of obdurate citizens.

Some instances may be cited. Saratov had always been a turbulent province — it was there that Stolypin had won his spurs as governor — and it sustained its reputation on this occasion. The socialist opposition felt the wrath of the soldiers as much or more than the bourgeoisie.[4] In Odessa, on the other hand, the Kadets bore the brunt of the soldiers' hostility.[5] In Kostroma

[1] As a soldier in Saratov put it, "Nothing matters except to end this damned war and get home" (quoted in the *Saratovskii Listok*, no. 241 [November 14, 1917]).

[2] *Russkiia Vedomosti*, no. 259 (November 26, 1917), where conditions in the Kozlov garrison are described in a letter; *Delo Naroda*, no. 214 (November 19, 1917), where a Menshevik protest against conditions in the XII Army is aired.

[3] This study is not concerned with the mechanics of voting. For the sake of clarity, however, it may be pointed out that there was no general ballot but rather a separate list of candidates for each party contesting the election in a given district (*okrug*). Each list bore a number, determined by the order of reception in the district in question. The voter was furnished with a list for each party, either by mail before the election or at the polling place upon demand. He chose the list of his preference and put it in an envelope, sealed the envelope and deposited it in the urn. The unwanted lists he discarded. The voter could choose only as between parties; once settled on a list, he had to take it as it was, not being able either to change the order of candidates or strike out a name. In Saratov some SR voters scratched Kerenski and had their ballots invalidated as a result (*Saratovskii Vestnik*, no. 245, November 15, 1917; *Saratovskii Listok*, no. 242, November 16, 1917). The "Belgian" or d'Hondt system of proportional representation was followed. See in general *Sputnik izbiratelia v Uchreditelnoe Sobranie* (Petrograd, 1917); simple explanations of voting system in *Russkoe Slovo*, no. 257 (November 24, 1917); *Delo Naroda*, no. 207 (November 12, 1917); more detailed explanation in O. A. Volkenstein, *Proportsionalnye vybory v Uchreditelnoe Sobranie* (Petrograd, 1917).

[4] *Saratovskii Listok*, no. 239 (November 11, 1917); *Saratovskii Vestnik*, no. 244 (November 14, 1917); report from Saratov in *Fakel*, no. 1 (November 25, 1917); report of Ina Rakitnikova in *Delo Naroda*, no. 232 (December 14, 1917).

[5] *Utro Rossii*, no. 261 (November 14, 1917).

province scenes reminiscent of tsarist times took place: soldiers arrived in the villages and behaved in challenging fashion, going everywhere armed and resorting freely to threats.[6] A priest in Riazañ province stated that when peasants' wives came to him to ask how to vote, they cast fearful glances over their shoulders, for Bolshevik soldiers had made the rounds of the village, declaring that everyone not voting their way would be known and would have his livestock, his grain, and his hut destroyed or taken away.[7] In Kozlov *uezd* of Tambov province agitators from the front sometimes threatened to kill their opponents.[8] For soldiers' wives they had a special argument: "If you don't vote for No. 7, just wait till your mate gets home — he'll beat the hell out of you!" [9]

But the offenses were not all on one side. The Bolsheviks had their grievances, too. It must be remembered that they did not control the electoral machinery, which carried over from the Provisional Government; and if they had the support of the highly articulate military element,[10] they also had the bitter opposition of other articulate elements, notably the schoolteachers, clergy, and kulaks. Though the schoolteacher was almost invariably an SR and the priest an adherent of the Kadet party or some other grouping still further to the right, they joined hands at times to

[6] Report on eve of the IV Congress, PSR, *Delo Naroda*, no. 220 (November 30, 1917).

[7] Alexander Drozdov, "Po Rossii: Slepaia Rossiia (Provintsialnyia vpechatleniia)," *Nash Vek*, no. 21 (December 23, 1917).

[8] *Russkiia Vedomosti*, no. 259 (November 26, 1917).

[9] See the informative correspondence from Kozlov, signed A. S., in *Delo Naroda*, no. 242 (December 28, 1917). The author is doubtlessly A[nastasia] S[lëtova], the wife of Chernov and in her own right one of the key figures in the SR organization in the black-earth zone, the center of party strength. She was one of the deputies elected from Tambov province. No. 7 was the Bolshevik list in that province.

[10] Not all the soldier propagandists, of course, agitated in favor of Bolshevism. Many worked for the PSR (see *ibid.* and N. Arepev, "Derevnia i Uchreditelnoe Sobranie," *Delo Naroda*, no. 236 (December 19, 1917); the latter describes the campaign in a canton of Tver province). But the SR soldiers seem to have lacked the verve and belligerence of their Bolshevik rivals. As for the Baltic sailors, they had a fanaticism all their own and were never anything except Bolshevik in sentiment.

combat the common enemy: thus in the village of Kandaurovka in Samara province the schoolmistress Bolshakova, with the aid of the local priest, forced the peasants to vote SR by snatching Bolshevik lists from their hands and by threatening their arrest in case of resistance; [11] while in a rural precinct of Pskov province the peasants — here apparently made of sterner stuff — chased the teacher away for having practiced deception at the polls (he was the presiding officer) and beat up the priest for having influenced the women in favor of the class enemy.[12] Bolshevik accounts of the election would not be Bolshevik if evil were not ascribed to those traditional scapegoats, the kulaks; yet there is no reason to doubt that the better-to-do peasants tried to turn the village against the party that menaced their class with extinction, using for that purpose means of suasion which ranged from subtle suggestion [13] to crude acts of physical violence — if we can believe the Soviet sources, one of which charges that in Saratov province peasants daring to vote the Bolshevik ticket were not infrequently beaten by the kulaks.[14] The Bolsheviks also suffered in other ways. Their agitation was trammeled or banned outright in some places, as in Spassko-Kashminskaia canton, Morshansk *uezd*, Tambov province, where the SR-dominated local administration justified its action on the grounds that the Bolsheviks were really German spies.[15] Another grievance was that something might happen to the party lists — their distribution might be delayed, or they might arrive in insufficient quantity, or they might never

[11] *Pravda*, no. 213 (December 13, 1917).

[12] *Derevenskaia Bednota*, no. 32 (November 18, 1917). The reverend father tore himself loose and ran away howling.

[13] See report from Pskov province, *ibid.*, no. 38 (November 25, 1917).

[14] V. P. Antonov-Saratovski, *Pod stiagom proletarskoi borby: Otryvki iz vospominanii o rabote v Saratove za vremia s 1915g. do 1918g.*, Vol. I (Moscow-Leningrad, 1925), p. 237. Sometimes the people were simply warned that the Bolsheviks were robbers and plunderers, and that those who followed them would be flogged with *nagaikas* (a Cossack's whip), as in 1905 — a reference to events still green in the memory of the Saratov peasantry.

[15] Report of G. Generalov, *Pravda*, no. 194 (November 19, 1917).

reach the voters at all.[16] The general effect in such cases was to leave the SR's a clear field for the election.

Hostilities were not confined to the Bolshevik and SR parties, and it is by no means necessary to rely solely on Bolshevik testimony for evidence of wrongdoing on the part of the opposition, particularly the SR opposition, composed as it was of so many self-righteous people. From the distant north comes a plaint from a peasant who adhered to the Kadet party, to the effect that the Ust-Sysolsk electoral commission of Vologda province, whose official duty it had been to explain all party programs to the voters, actually had carried out its mission in such a one-sided manner as to rig the election in favor of the PSR. In this work of perversion, the propagandists dispatched to the villages in the guise of official instructors had the full coöperation of the local authorities, who refused to give out the programs of other parties and demanded support for their own.[17] Down in the Ukraine, in fertile Poltava province, the Selianska Spilka or "Village Union," a powerful organization completely dominated by the Ukrainian Socialist Revolutionaries, had been guilty of excesses in its campaign against the Landowners' or Farmers' party, the lists of which were suppressed and its representatives excluded from the local electoral commissions.[18] Sometimes matters were carried to the point of terrorism, for we read that in Sokiriantsy village the

[16] *Izvestiia Moskovskago Soveta*, no. 232 (December 16, 1917), which cites instances of delay until the very day of the election in rural districts of Pskov, Vologda, Viatka, and Vitebsk provinces; *Pravda*, no. 200 (November 26, 1917), no. 208 (December 7, 1917). For abuses committed at the expense of the Bolsheviks, see in general *Pravda*, no. 202 (November 30, 1917), no. 3 (January 5, 1918); N. Rubinstein, *Bolsheviki i Uchreditelnoe Sobranie* (n.p., 1938), pp. 51–52; AOR, *Vserossiiskoe Uchreditelnoe Sobranie*, pp. 209–210, n. 12.

[17] Letter of Ilarion Sharapov, *Severnoe Ekho*, no. 99 (December 20, 1917). This newspaper was published in Vologda and was Kadet in tone if not in affiliation.

[18] Generally referred to as *zemlevladeltsy* (landowners), the adherents of this movement in the Ukraine are more frequently termed *khleboroby*, the proper translation of which is "farmers." There were more real farmers, of course, in the Ukraine than in Great Russia (farmers, that is, in the sense of peasant proprietors).

priest had suffered indignities — he was locked in jail, struck on the nose, and threatened with being torn to pieces — all because he belonged to the Landowners' party.[19] There were instances when peasants appeared before the authorities and begged on bended knees for some paper certifying that they were not members of the hated party; otherwise, they declared, their lives would be in danger.[20] Thus the use of nefarious tactics was by no means restricted to the Bolshevik party.

And yet side by side with this record of intimidation and violence another record could be compiled, bearing witness to the fact that in many places the voting passed off smoothly and without serious infractions of the electoral code. Let us take the case of the big cities. In Petrograd the outstanding feature of the election was its humdrum character. There was no especial enthusiasm, and no marked excesses, aside from the Red Guard's descent on the offices of the *Rech* the night of November 12.[21] A total absence of violence was noted in certain sections of the city — Moskovski, Liteinyi, Spasski, Vasilevski — and if local sentiment made it impossible for the Kadets to campaign on the Vyborg side,[22] they were very active in the Kazanski district; while along the Kriukov Canal even monarchist agitation could be observed.[23] The central organ of the PSR, the *Delo Naroda*, is hard put to find something wrong with the election; thus it ascribes a privileged position in the pre-electoral campaign to the Bolsheviks because of their monopoly of motor transport, only to contradict itself in the very same issue by speaking of automobiles in the service of the Kadets.[24] Even more impressive is the record in Moscow, where the fairness of the election is attested by all sources without exception. The Menshevik organ conceded that

[19] A reading of the record leads one to the conclusion that priests must have had a hard time of it during this election.

[20] D., "Vybory v Poltavskoi gubernii," *Nash Vek*, no. 18 (December 20, 1917).

[21] The *Rech* was the central organ of the Kadet party.

[22] A proletarian center and stronghold of Bolshevism.

[23] *Delo Naroda*, nos. 208, 209 (November 13, 14, 1917).

[24] See "Na ulitse," in *ibid.*, no. 208.

no ground existed for contesting the election,[25] and even the conservative *Russkoe Slovo*, while duly noting certain minor disorders
at the polls, was constrained to admit that the Kadets enjoyed
full civic rights and were able to contend on virtually even terms
with the dominant party.[26] This is a remarkable circumstance in
view of the hard fighting that had attended the October Revolution in Moscow and the blood-letting so recently past. Not only
from the metropolitan centers but also from the country at large
come reports of a quiet and orderly election. From Kostroma in
the north to the Crimea in the south, from the Roumanian Front
in the west to Vladivostok on the Pacific — from Tver, Tula,
Minsk, Kiev, Podolia, Odessa, Ekaterinoslav province, Tambov,
Penza, Samara, Simbirsk, Kazañ, Perm, Kars, Erivan, Tomsk,
Irkutsk, and Blagoveshchensk — come accounts of normal conditions of voting.[27]

How, then, are we to reconcile this welter of conflicting evidence? A careful consideration of all the factors involved leads
inevitably to the conclusion that the normal aspects of the election far outweigh the irregularities, numerous though these may
be. Overshadowing everything else is the circumstance that the
Bolsheviks had the power and lost the election. The results speak
for themselves. There is not the slightest evidence on the government's part of a master plan to subvert the election or falsify the
returns. The indubitable freedom of voting in the large cities
shows that Lenin's regime did not intend to overawe the voters
where it had the physical means of doing so, and elsewhere it was
too newly established and administratively too weak to have
done this even had it desired. True, there was a huge Bolshevik

[25] *Klich*, no. 1 (November 23, 1917).

[26] No. 255 (November 21, 1917). See also the account in *Russkiia Vedomosti*, no. 255 (November 21, 1917), and the report telephoned to Petrograd
in *Delo Naroda*, no. 215 (November 21, 1917).

[27] *Delo Naroda*, nos. 209, 211, 212, 214, 218 (November 14, 16, 17, 19,
24, 1917); Sviatitski in *ibid.*, no. 227 (December 8, 1917); *Russkoe Slovo*,
nos. 255, 257 (November 21, 24, 1917); *Volia Narodnaia*, no. 1 (November
28, 1917); *Izvestiia Vserossiiskoi po delam o vyborakh v Uchreditelnoe Sobranie Komissii*, no. 21 (November 22, 1917), p. 15, and no. 22 (November
29, 1917), p. 32.

vote both in Petrograd and in Moscow, but in neither city did it reach quite 50 per cent of the total, and few would contend that the percentages attained were excessive as a measure of strength of this proletarian party in the chief proletarian centers of the empire.

Furthermore, the record of fraud and violence on close inspection is not impressive. Of actual breakdowns in the conduct of the election (aside from postponements due to technical difficulties) we hear almost nothing — the only clear-cut instance of soldiers' interference breaking up the election is in Salopinski canton of Kaluga province — an area so small as not to merit consideration.[28] There were very few slayings, considering the extent of the country and the size of the population. The chairman of the Krasnikovo electoral commission in Orël province was killed by soldiers when he tried to restrain their illegal actions; [29] another such official, in this case a priest, was slain in Pskov province; [30] the Menshevik mayor of Bakhmut lost his life under circumstances that were not explained in the press [31] — and that was about all. As many fatalities have occurred at election time in the single state of Kentucky.

For the most part attempts at intimidation seem to have stopped at oral threats; they were spontaneous and sporadic, and without marked effect on the results. In turbulent Saratov province the Bolsheviks lost to the SR's by a ratio better than 2:1; [32] the fact that they did relatively well in this black-earth district was due not merely to the strong-armed tactics of the Saratov garrison, but also to the presence of a first-class industrial center, the city of Tsaritsyn, now known as Stalingrad. Though Kozlov *uezd*

---

[28] *Delo Naroda*, no. 212 (November 17, 1917). In addition, the SR organ accused the Bolsheviks of disrupting the election in Rzhëv *uezd* of Tver province (*ibid.*, no. 218, November 24, 1917), but it is not clear what happened in that locality.

[29] *Russkiia Vedomosti*, no. 253 (November 18, 1917); *Sovremennost*, no. 1 (November 23, 1917); *Utro Rossii*, no. 265 (November 18, 1917).

[30] *Sovremennost*, no. 1 (November 23, 1917).

[31] *Fakel*, no. 1 (November 25, 1917).

[32] See Chapter II, note 4.

of Tambov province, as we have seen, counted a large number of soldier propagandists who threatened to deal out death to their opponents, and no less than fifty of the redoubtable Baltic sailors who preached the same fiery message of Bolshevism, the degree of actual violence was small, much smaller than would have been necessary to save the government party from a decisive beating.[33] According to another source, the reaction of the peasantry here varied in the face of such provocation, the entire population in some villages bowing to force and casting only Bolshevik ballots, whereas in others like Tarbeev the inhabitants beat the Bolshevik bullies and threw them out of the polling place.[34] Both sources agree that in some places the Bolsheviks beat their foes, and in others were beaten by them. Here in a *uezd* out in the sticks we probably have in microcosm a true picture of what was going on all over Russia, the violence and pressure on one side being offset by similar tactics on the other, the result being a balanced election. There probably is a residue of illegality, however, on the side of the Bolsheviks, but not a large enough one to influence materially the outcome.

Nor was that outcome affected to any appreciable extent by the more subtle means of swinging an election such as are practiced in Western lands — illegal voting, stuffing the ballot box, falsification of returns, and so on. Undoubtedly some double-voting took place, particularly in the case of garrison troops,[35] and here and there protests were voiced at the theft or suppression of ballots — as by the Mensheviks at Motovilikha in the Urals,[36]

[33] Letter of A[nastasia] S[lëtova], *Delo Naroda*, no. 242 (December 28, 1917).

[34] *Russkiia Vedomosti*, no. 259 (November 26, 1917).

[35] See the warning proclamation of Mayor Shreider of Petrograd in *Vestnik gorodskogo samoupravleniia* (*Vedomosti Petrogradskago Gradonachalstva*), no. 118(203) (November 12, 1917). Soldiers were not infrequently provided with more than one qualifying certificate because of confusion about their home and military addresses. See also "Vybornyia nedorazumeniia," *Russkoe Slovo*, no. 255 (November 21, 1917).

[36] *Klich*, no. 1 (November 23, 1917). Here there was a big nest of Bolsheviks (Motovilikha is an industrial suburb of Perm).

or by the rightists in a village of Kostroma province [37] — but these were strictly isolated incidents and, all told, would add up to relatively little. Only in the case of Smolensk was a district electoral commission so thoroughly dissatisfied with conditions under which voting took place as to pose the question of a reëlection.[38]

The best evidence of the basic soundness of the returns is afforded by the controversy that arose in the capital between the Council of People's Commissars and the All-Russian Electoral Commission. Apparently the Bolsheviks, or at least some of their leaders, expected to come out ahead with the help of the Left SR's [39] until they saw the handwriting on the wall as returns from the black-earth zone began pouring in during the second week of the balloting. They realized then that most of the SR deputies would adhere to the centrist or right-wing factions of that huge but disintegrating party; [40] they were seized with alarm and, shrilly accusing the Commission of falsification and other abuses, decreed its arrest on November 23, only to release it a few days later without having substantiated the charges.[41] Thereafter a commission of surveillance was set up under Uritski and the

[37] *Russkoe Slovo*, no. 257 (November 24, 1917).

[38] *Delo Naroda*, no. 213 (November 18, 1917).

[39] See statement of Lunacharski, quoted in *ibid.*, no. 209 (November 14, 1917).

[40] The Bolsheviks never made any distinction between the numerically preponderant center under Chernov and the influential right wing, friendly to Kerenski; both were lumped together as "right SR's."

[41] It is interesting to note that on the preceding day a report had been received from Oboian *uezd*, Kursk province, crediting the SR's with 70,000 votes and the Bolsheviks with only 3,000 (*ibid.*, no. 216, November 22, 1917). This was the first decisive indication of how the vote would go in the populous black-earth region. The early returns were nearly all from towns and the Bolsheviks had been ahead. Then the rural returns began to accumulate and by November 26 the SR's were in the lead. See country-wide totals in the *Russkoe Slovo*, no. 259 and *passim*.

It may be added that the charges against the Commission have never been substantiated. For refutation of charges see *Delo Naroda*, nos. 228, 229 (December 9, 10, 1917). Full account of the affair may be found in *Izvestiia Vserossiiskoi po delam o vyborakh v Uchreditelnoe Sobranie Komissii*, no. 22 (November 29, 1917), pp. 1–28.

bickering continued, the assembling of returns now being more difficult than ever, but since the returns received continued to be as unfavorable to the Bolsheviks as before, the conclusion is inescapable that neither the All-Russian Commission nor the Soviet authorities were guilty of falsification.

On the basis of all the available evidence, therefore, it is safe to say that the first criterion of a valid election has been met in this instance: although a good many voters were subjected to intimidation in one form or another, and what went into the urns was not always what came out, the vast majority of the electorate freely exercised the right of suffrage and could be sure that its ballots would be counted as cast. It was far from being a model election, but it certainly was not a farce.

CHAPTER V

THE QUESTION OF VALIDITY: DID THE PEOPLE KNOW WHAT THEY WERE DOING?

WE ARE NOW READY for the second criterion — the consciousness of the voting public. Here we are in deep water from the outset, owing to the intangible character of some of the factors involved, the prejudice exhibited on every hand, the absence of real illumination amid an ocean of verbiage, and — worst of all — the silence of the records on certain crucial matters. Loquaciousness would hardly be what it is if it did not flow where it is not needed and were not shut off where it would be welcome.

The view has been expressed that the results of the election to the All-Russian Constituent Assembly were somehow not representative of the Russian people, that the Russian peasant was innately a conservative creature who would have supported the Church and the Tsar, or at the very least the Kadets, had his mind not been befuddled by the fumes of revolutionary propaganda. The essence of the Constitutional Democratic program — the combination of a belief in universal suffrage with defense of the institution of private property — was predicated upon this assumption. And the Union of Monarchists proclaimed soon after the results became known that it would never recognize the authority of a body chosen under conditions of fraud and violence, in the absence of which a monarchist majority would have been assured.[1] At the other end of the political spectrum, and equally scornful of the results, are the Bolsheviks, one of whose leaders has asserted that a delay of even a month in holding the election would have permitted his party, through further intensive

---

[1] See comment of N. S. Rusanov, "Chernaia sotnia i krasnaia," *Delo Naroda*, no. 221 (December 1, 1917); "Chernaia sotnia shevelitsia," *Izvestiia Tsentralnago Ispolnitelnago Komiteta i petrogradskago soveta*, no. 240 (November 30, 1917), p. 4.

cultivation of the peasantry, to secure control of the Assembly.[2] Sweeping assertions of this sort, insofar as they do not rest upon wishful thinking, are based upon two widely observed phenomena in 1917: first, a startling fluctuation of party strength in the towns and, second, the success enjoyed by divergent groups in propagandizing the peasants. In the first case the inference is that the parties had no following in the true sense of the word, and in the second, that the country population resembled a flock of sheep which could be herded in any direction. Let us now examine critically each of these phenomena, after which we may be able to determine whether or not the detractors of the election are justified in their contentions.

The shifting of votes from one political camp to another attained truly formidable proportions and occurred in an amazingly short interval of time. It is to be seen in a comparison of the results in local elections with those of the general election to the Constituent Assembly and is restricted to the towns, for it is impossible to measure sentiment in the village before the November balloting. The outstanding example is the city of Moscow, where the SR's swept the field in the June vote for the central municipal council, only to sustain a catastrophic defeat in the September election to municipal district councils, followed by the final rout in November (see accompanying tabulation).[3]

[2] Antonov, *Pod stiagom proletarskoi borby*, I, 238. See also Uritski's report to the Petrograd Bolshevik Committee in L. Trotski, *Sochineniia* (Moscow, n.d.), III, Part II, 364, 367. Uritski contended that the new regime had not had enough time to get its program across to the population in more remote parts of the country. But for this, it would have secured "at least a majority."

[3] Table of comparison in *Russkiia Vedomosti*, no. 257 (November 24, 1917). As only round figures are given, it is not reproduced here. The figures given here are from the following sources: June election, *Russkoe Slovo*, no. 149 (July 2, 1917); September election, *ibid.*, no. 222 (September 29, 1917); November election, *Russkiia Vedomosti*, no. 257 (November 24, 1917).

Party	June	September	November
SR	374,885	54,374	62,260
Bolshevik	75,409	198,320	366,148
Kadet	108,781	101,106	263,859
Menshevik	76,407	15,887	21,597
Others	11,086	16,160	50,899
Total vote	646,568	385,847	764,763

Expressed in terms of percentage, the vote for the major parties was as follows:

Party	June	September	November
SR	58	14	8
Bolshevik	12	51	48
Kadet	17	26	35
Menshevik	12	4	3

In Petrograd the same tendency is apparent, though not to the same degree: [4]

Party	August	November
SR	205,666	152,230
Bolshevik	183,694	424,027
Kadet	114,485	246,506
Menshevik	23,552	29,167
Others	21,982	90,403
Total vote ..	549,379	942,333

What kind of an electorate was it that could give a party an absolute majority in June and then slash its vote to 14 per cent in September and 8 per cent in November? Is it possible even to speak of political consciousness in the face of such a demonstra-

[4] Figures for August election to city council from *Delo Naroda*, no. 136 (August 25, 1917); November figures from *ibid.*, nos. 211, 212 (November 16, 17, 1917). In May the district or ward councils had been filled (the order was the reverse of that in Moscow). Because of bloc voting and diffusion of returns, however, it is not possible to give a clear picture of party strength in the May election.

tion of political volatility? In Saratov it had been only less catastrophic than in Moscow: the moderate socialists had seen their following shrink from 37,564 in July to 12,798 in November, a loss of a good two-thirds; more than 10,000 voters had deserted to the "bourgeois" camp, and within the socialist fold itself, nearly 15,000 had switched their allegiance to Bolshevism.[5] As the Saratov editor observed, these floaters were not really adherents of socialism or, indeed, of anything else and hence could not be ascribed to the party of their momentary choice; only the Popular Socialists had possessed a stable following from summer to fall, and that a very small one. Where no stability of partisan sympathies obtained, there could be no talk of political consciousness.[6]

And yet what had happened was typical of any revolution: the decomposition of the center and the building up of the extremes as the revolution deepened. From the swamp of political repression the Russian citizen had emerged onto the stream of political freedom, and it was necessary for him to get his bearings, identifying himself with one or the other of the unfamiliar objects suddenly appearing on the surface. As the stream was flowing so swiftly, it is not surprising that he floundered about, grasping first at one support and then at another. The early elections had taken place on a local scale and during the honeymoon stage of the revolution. What more splendid receptacle could have been provided for the votes of bewildered citizens, their hearts filled with enthusiasm and their heads with nebulous ideas, than the Socialist Revolutionary party? But the revolution wore on and the honeymoon spirit wore off; the passions loosed by Kornilov's August rebellion and Lenin's October Revolution tore the mask of romanticism from the face of the class struggle, and the urban masses lurched to the right or the left, parting the center and clearing the field for civil war. The ranks of Bolshevism swelled and likewise those

[5] The comparison here requires no adjustment, as the total vote is almost identical (60,025 in the July municipal election and 60,182 in November).

[6] *Saratovskii Vestnik*, no. 248 (November 18, 1917).

of Constitutional Democracy, establishing for the first time a kind of political equilibrium among parties that rested on a solid contingent of voters who would not desert at the next turn of the revolutionary wheel. It is true that Bolshevism numbered among its adherents many who went with the victor of the hour — the bandwagon vote, in other words — and that the Kadets sheltered elements of the right — perhaps very substantial elements — but each party had an irreducible core of strength which no doubt accounted for most of its following. Thus it was not the election to the Constituent Assembly but rather the earlier local elections which had registered an ephemeral sentiment; by November the lines had hardened, and the voters knew much better what they were doing than in preceding tests of sentiment.[7]

But what of the village? The able editor at Saratov had wrung his hands at the mere thought of it, exclaiming that if the electorate of a city called the "Athens of the Volga" could put on such an exhibition of political irresponsibility, then what must be the situation out in the country, amid the dark, dumb mass of the peasantry? The rustics, as we know, had favored the SR ticket. Was this merely an evidence of the customary lag of the village behind the town, or did it have some independent meaning? Sources of varied political inclination attest to the ease with which the peasant was influenced in 1917. To the reader it almost seems that whoever approached him last received his vote. The testimony is unanimous that soldiers swayed the mass at will and exerted a profound influence on the outcome of the election. Thus in the almost exclusively agrarian province of Chernigov the Bolshevik party, with no organization at all in most of the *uezds* and only a feeble one in others, nevertheless gained authority in

[7] The election figures for Moscow show that by fall the Bolshevik following had become stabilized. Not only did the October Revolution fail to increase the relative strength of the party — it could not even avert the loss of the absolute majority secured in September, the vote falling from 51 to 48 per cent. Although the opposition seized on this circumstance, it was of little significance in view of the much larger turnout at the polls (virtually a 100 per cent increase over September). It does minimize, however, the effect of the bandwagon vote.

the eyes of the people and received more than a quarter of a million votes in November as a tribute to the zeal of soldiers returning from the front.[8] The same phenomenon is observed in widely separated parts of the country.[9] These men from the front were as ubiquitous in the rear as their actions were energetic; not even central Siberia was spared their visitations.[10] A beautiful example of their influence is reported from Viazma: cantons near the railroad line went for the Bolsheviks and those further away for the SR's, simply because soldiers had worked the villages near the stations but had not penetrated into the interior.[11] Sometimes, as in the Moscow industrial region, workers would take the place of soldiers, going by droves into the backwoods with the message of Bolshevism and presenting their party with an unexpected victory in unlikely places.[12] Only the shortage of propagandists circumscribed the scope of the victory, so fruitful were the results of agitation, for all that was needed was to talk to the simple folk in order to win them over.[13] The mood of the peasantry could easily be changed, if we are to judge from what happened in several cantons of Tver province, where a single agitator dispelled the animosity to Bolshevism and won the populace over to his cause.[14] At times the peasants betrayed their past by wanting

[8] V. K. Shcherbakov, *Zhovtneva revoliutsiia i roki gromadianskoï borotbi na Chernigivshchini* (Chernigov, 1927), pp. 33–34 (written in Ukrainian).

[9] *Novaia Zhizn*, no. 201 (December 14, 1917), report from Minsk; *Delo Naroda*, no. 220 (November 30, 1917), report from Kostroma; *ibid.*, no. 231 (December 13, 1917), report from Moscow province; *Pravda*, no. 194 (November 19, 1917), report from Kaluga; see *Russkoe Slovo*, no. 255 (November 21, 1917), for general comment.

[10] *Utro Rossii*, no. 279 (December 6, 1917); *Izvestiia Vserossiiskoi po delam o vyborakh v Uchreditelnoe Sobranie Komissii*, no. 21 (November 22, 1917), p. 15, citing reports of pressure exerted by soldiers in the Krasnoiarsk district.

[11] *Russkiia Vedomosti*, no. 258 (November 25, 1917).

[12] N. Meshcheriakov in *Izvestiia Moskovskago Soveta*, no. 217 (November 29, 1917).

[13] *Moskovskaia provintsiia v semnadtsatom godu*, ed. E. Popova (Moscow-Leningrad, 1927), pp. 154–155.

[14] "Vesti iz provintsii," *Derevenskaia Bednota*, no. 38 (November 25, 1917). Yet side by side with this must be set evidence of a contradictory nature from still another canton in the same province: here a public

to be told how to vote,[15] and the inhabitants of one village, deciding that they had made a mistake, upbraided the authorities for having failed to send instructions: "Why weren't we, dark and ignorant people, told for whom to vote?" [16]

Is there no evidence whatever of a will of its own on the part of the Russian peasantry? And what if it were subjected simultaneously to opposing stimuli — how then would it react? Unfortunately, we have no real illumination of the temper of the village as it approached the urns, or of how it cast its vote. Scraps of information may painfully be put together, but the countless villages of Russia are the great dark province of the election. In the case of Kozlov *uezd* of Tambov province, however, conditions have been analyzed by a prominent political figure who was honest and intelligent; returns are available which are adequate if not complete; and location is such as to make it a typical constituency in the black-earth zone, where most of the Russian people have lived since the close of the seventeenth century. To afford a graphic illustration of the contrast between town and country, the figures for the *uezd* center, the town of Kozlov, are given alongside those of the *uezd* itself, exclusive of the town: [17]

---

meeting (*skhod*) had been called at the insistence of a Smolny agitator, and he was listened to, but the literature he passed out was torn up and the canton gave the SR's 12,000 votes to 1,400 for the Bolsheviks. Perhaps the explanation of his failure lies in the fact that in this locality soldiers returning from the front generally recommended the SR list (N. Arepev, "Derevnia i Uchreditelnoe Sobranie," *Delo Naroda*, no. 236, December 19, 1917).

[15] Al. Altaev, "Kak prokhodiat vybory v Uchreditelnoe Sobranie v derevne," *Derevenskaia Bednota*, no. 32 (November 18, 1917).

[16] Letter from Podoskliaia village, Nizhne-Spassk canton, Tambov *uezd*, to the *Tambovskii Zemskii Vestnik*, quoted in *Russkoe Slovo*, no. 247 (November 10, 1917). They had voted for the Coöperatives' list and now favored the SR's. Something is wrong, for it is stated that the balloting occurred on October 22, and November 12 (25) was the first day of voting. The author knows of no instance of voting before that date, albeit of plenty after it. Maybe the village jumped the gun.

[17] Town figures, *Russkoe Slovo*, no. 252 (November 17, 1917); *uezd* figures, *ibid.*, no. 256 (November 23, 1917).

		Town		Uezd
	Civilian	*Garrison*	*Total*	
Registered	19,608	8,046	27,654	?
Voted	9,467	4,045	13,512	137,901
SR	?	?	1,642	96,033
Bolshevik	908	3,006	3,914	35,224
Kadet	?	?	5,107	2,997
Menshevik	?	?	1,902	1,856
Popular Socialist	?	?	⎫	366
Landowner	?	?	947 ⎬	1,288
Mohammedan	?	?	⎭	137? [18]

Here on a scale smaller and therefore more revealing than for
the provinces given before, the basic structure of the election is
laid bare. The Kadets carried the town, but were swamped in the
garrison and buried in the village. The Bolsheviks had the support
of the peasants in uniform but not of those who were rooted in
the soil. Nevertheless, this party of the proletariat had achieved a
considerable following in a purely non-proletarian area, faring
much better in the villages than in the town proper. How had
these results been brought about? Certainly not by force and repression, the local aspects of which have already been considered.
It is not necessary to conjecture in this instance — we know what
happened. The parties had carried on a campaign that was not
only free but rigorous. With the aid of secondary school students,
who were middle class in background and nationalist in sentiment,
the Kadets had made a strong bid for votes in the town, getting
their campaign under way long before the twelfth of November.
Their placards could be seen everywhere. But out in the country
they made no headway whatever; there the SR's and the Bolsheviks held the field and no other party had even so much as a
look-in. The fierce and prolonged agitation of the Bolshevik
soldiers and sailors was not without its effect — the SR leader
tells us that the people hearkened to their simple message, "he

[18] Difference between announced total vote and sum of vote by parties.
May represent an error or may be vote cast for Moslem list, which is
omitted from tabulation.

who is for peace, let him vote for us" — but on the whole they fought in vain against the intrenched position of the PSR with its manifold roots in the Tambov countryside,[19] its old and tested ties with the peasantry, and its corps of veteran workers. The SR's countered the soldiers' propaganda by bringing in their own men from the front, and party supporters in the trenches wrote home, advising their relatives to choose the SR list. In this manner the all-powerful influence of the front was divided and arrayed against itself. The election on the whole passed off normally: no one was killed and of the few who were beaten, some were on one side and some on the other.[20]

What happened, then, is reasonably clear. In this sleepy provincial town of Kozlov, a trading center with little industry and no proletariat to speak of, the Kadets had staged a determined effort under the very nose of the garrison and had achieved a large plurality. As in Petrograd and Moscow, the middle class had given them its vote. But that was all. Their activity did not extend beyond the town for the very simple reason there was no social element they could appeal to except the landowners. They had nothing to say to the peasants that the peasants wanted to hear. The Russian village was invincibly determined to have the land of the nobility and pay nothing for it, and the stand of the Kadets for compensation, however justified it may have been legally or morally, had no other effect than to erect an insuperable barrier to party work in the village.[21] It did no good to argue the rights of private property — there was no class of peasant

---

[19] Here the foundations of the party had been laid by V. M. Chernov, his wife, A. N. Slëtova, his brother-in-law, Stephen Slëtov, and their associates in the last decade of the preceding century. See Chernov, *Zapiski sotsialista-revoliutsionera,* Book I (Berlin, Petersburg and Moscow, 1922), pp. 249*ff.*

[20] Account of A[nastasia] S[lëtova] in *Delo Naroda,* no. 242 (December 28, 1917).

[21] One illustration of this: the peasants in Subochinskaia canton, Petrograd province, shouted down a Kadet speaker who attempted to present his party's program. The Bolshevik agitator overcame his SR rivals; the Kadet was not even heard (*Derevenskaia Bednota,* no. 38, November 25, 1917).

proprietors, no farming element, to appreciate such arguments. The Kadets lost the village, not because of the revolution, but because of the heritage of the old regime. Nothing kept them from the village except the temper of the village itself.

If the SR's could easily outbid the Kadets for the peasants' favor, the Bolsheviks could go beyond the SR's. They could tax their rivals with delaying the land reform and they could promise an immediate end to war. Slëtova tells us that for the most part the Bolsheviks got their votes from the villages near town (*pri-gorodnyia sëla*) and from the women; [22] although she does not explain why this was so, we may readily conjecture that the villages near town were those most worked over by the garrison, and that the women wanted to get their men home from the front. So there were thousands and thousands of peasant votes for Lenin's party, but the mass still preferred the party which first had brought it the message of Land and Liberty and which it knew from old association.

That the peasantry was vitally interested in the election is attested by the extraordinarily high turnout at the polls. The degree of participation in the *uezd* as a whole stood at 86 per cent and in some cantons it exceeded 90 per cent — figures that cannot be matched in any free election in the West and that are scarcely surpassed in a dictator's plebescite. The mood of the village was solemn and exalted as it prepared to vote: though the villagers would not listen for a moment to the political advice of the priest, they were not ready to dispense with the services of his cult, and so the church bells were rung and a *Te Deum* celebrated, after which virtually the whole population thronged to the polling-place, it mattered not that the weather was miserable and the roads were out. The enthusiasm of the rural population stands in striking contrast to the apathy of the townspeople, less than half of whom

[22] She states that secrecy of the ballot was a farce in the village; everyone knew what everyone else was going to do. In addition to the women, the village youth appears to have furnished many recruits for Bolshevism; at least that was the impression of an eye-witness in Riazañ province (Drozdov, "Po Rossii: Slepaia Rossiia [Provintsialnyia vpechat-leniia]," *Nash Vek*, no. 21, December 23, 1917).

took the trouble to vote; even the garrison, about whose activity we hear so much, made only a mediocre showing.

We may conclude from the evidence at hand that there was nothing fundamentally wrong with the election in Kozlov *uezd*. When burghers vote for property rights, soldiers and their wives for peace and demobilization, and peasants for land, what is there about the spectacle that is abnormal or unreal? True, comprehension of party programs was rudimentary and attachment to party names perfunctory, but in an elemental way the electorate knew what it was doing. The degree of consciousness was not high, but it is foolish to contend that none existed.

The question now arises of how typical Kozlov *uezd* was of Russia as a whole. The answer is that it affords a cross-section of the black-earth zone but not necessarily of other regions. The peasantry of the black earth offered sterner resistance to Bolshevism than the peasantry elsewhere, partly because the black-earth peasantry had only agrarian interests — in contrast to the mixed, half-peasant, half-proletarian class in the north — and partly because Social Revolutionism here on its home soil possessed a tradition and an organizational continuity with the past which made it a force to be reckoned with and enabled it to hold its lines much better than in other parts of the country where it resembled nothing so much as a mushroom, grown up overnight in the fetid atmosphere of 1917. The more sustained character of the party struggle here in the bread-basket of Russia imparts greater meaning to the election.

In other respects, however, Kozlov was representative of all sections of the country. In towns that were administrative or trading centers with little or no industrial life, it was not only frequently but usually the case for the Kadets to come out on top, and even the Mensheviks, who clung to the euphemistic title of United Social Democrats, not infrequently ran ahead of their Bolshevik rivals. It was not so much the weakness of these parties in the towns as the weakness of the towns in Russia which accounted for their poor showing. The garrisons, on the other hand, were nearly always strongholds of Bolshevism, and many a town would have registered an overwhelming defeat for that party had it not been saved by the soldiers' votes.[23] The same disproportion between the turnout in town and country that obtained in Kozlov *uezd* could be observed throughout the empire, though not always to the same degree. Nearly everywhere the town population [24] seemed dispirited and disillusioned in the Constituent Assembly, as though having a presentiment of what lay in store for that body after the October Revolution. The country people, however, still believed in the institution they thought would give them the land and attended the polls in great numbers, bringing with them the aged and the blind and voting with a lift of spirit unobserved elsewhere.[25] In the towns the portion of the electorate participating rarely rose as high as 70 per cent, usually did not exceed 50 per cent, and sometimes sank as low as 30 per cent, whereas in the country a participation of 60 to 80 per cent was the rule and even 90 per cent was not unknown. As a consequence, the normally vast preponderance of the village became vaster still.[26]

Thus the information pertaining to Kozlov *uezd* affords much insight into the character and conduct of the election, not only for that large portion of Russia comprising the black-earth zone but for other regions as well. There is one bit of information lacking, however, and it is of crucial importance. A dispatch in the

[23] Boris Nikolaevski, "Pervye itogi," *Klich*, no. 1 (November 23, 1917); *Fakel*, no. 1 (November 25, 1917); "Vybory v Uchreditelnoe Sobranie," *Russkiia Vedomosti*, no. 257 (November 24, 1917).

[24] The metropolitan centers are to some extent an exception. There the class struggle raged unabated and the attendance at the polls was better, reaching 65.4 per cent in Moscow and 71 per cent in Petrograd. It was the working class, however, that evinced the most interest; the middle class, and also the soldiers, lagged behind (*Delo Naroda*, nos. 209, 210, 212 [November 14, 15, 17, 1917]; *Volnost*, no. 25 [November 17, 1917]; *Russkoe Slovo*, no. 255 [November 21, 1917]).

[25] N. Arepev, "Derevnia i Uchreditelnoe Sobranie," *Delo Naroda*, no. 236 (December 19, 1917); *Russkoe Slovo*, no. 255 (November 21, 1917); *Novaia Zhizn*, no. 201 (December 14, 1917), report of Minsk correspondent; *Saratovskii Vestnik*, no. 252 (November 24, 1917), noting contrast in Khvalynsk *uezd*.

[26] *Russkiia Vedomosti*, no. 263 (December 1, 1917).

Russkiia Vedomosti, citing with approval the example of peasants who beat their tormenters and chased them from the polls, asserts that unfortunately such courage was not always forthcoming, and that in some villages the entire population bowed to threats and cast only Bolshevik ballots.[27] Are we to infer that the reverse was also true, and that in many villages hostile to Bolshevism only SR ballots were cast? If so, in how many? In Kozlov *uezd* 96,033 votes were recorded for the SR's and 35,224 for the Bolsheviks, a ratio of nearly 3:1. What does that mean? Does it mean that in the average village three of the inhabitants voted SR for every one that voted Bolshevik? Or does it mean that in four villages of approximately equal size, three voted solidly SR and one voted solidly Bolshevik? Could the Russian peasant exercise the right of suffrage as an individual or only as a member of a herd? In short, was this a genuine election, or only a measurement of the relative effect of divergent pressures playing upon an inert mass?

Unfortunately, such conjectures can not be dismissed as idle speculation. Besides the instance mentioned, there are other indications of herd voting. We are told that the rural population in the Taganrog area was all but unanimous in its support of the PSR.[28] Even more impressive is the testimony from Oboian *uezd* of Kursk province to the effect that entire cantons cast nothing but SR votes (in the *uezd* as a whole the Bolsheviks had only 3,000 and the Kadets 1,000 against 70,000 for the SR's).[29] The village commune in Great Russia functioned collectively in many ways; may it not have done so in regard to voting, especially when we consider that going to the polls appears to have been more a community than an individual affair?[30] Sometimes the peasants in a village declared they had made their choice and did

[27] No. 259 (November 26, 1917).

[28] *Klich*, no. 1 (November 23, 1917); *Delo Naroda*, no. 218 (November 24, 1917), which claims 95 per cent of the vote for the SR's.

[29] *Delo Naroda*, no. 216 (November 22, 1917).

[30] Arepev gives an interesting account of the electoral scene in a canton of Tver province (in *ibid.*, no. 236, December 19, 1917).

not wish to listen to any other party.[31] Yet the only two illumi-
nating accounts we have of what went on in the village at the time
of the election do not suggest that the vote was undivided. It
was not the collective will of the village but the individual choice
of the head of the household which decided the issue in the un-
named canton of Tver province; the other members of the household, as a rule, simply followed his example.[32] And the inference
to be drawn from Slëtova's report on Kozlov *uezd* is that the votes
of soldiers' wives, if nothing else, provided an element of dissent
in SR villages.

But what of the returns themselves? What light do they shed
on the subject of herd voting as a means of determining the level
of political consciousness of the Russian village? It is precisely
here that the investigator encounters a blank wall. There are no
returns by villages. They are announced for towns, provinces,
uezds, and in some cases for cantons, but even that does not help,
for a canton consists of a number of villages and hence could give
the appearance of a mixed vote even though certain villages might
have gone all one way and others all the other way. Neither
Sviatitski, nor Lenin, nor the Archives of the October Revolution
give a single example of how the village voted, and one searches
in vain through the maze of figures in the metropolitan press of
1917 for a clue to the solution of this question on which the whole
character of the election hinges. In one single instance the central
organ of the PSR printed the returns for a rural precinct in
Simferopol *uezd*, Taurida province (the Crimea), not bothering
to give the name of the precinct but being content to let the
figures speak for themselves: [33]

SR	586
Bolshevik	1
Kadet	2
Mohammedan	53

[31] *Moskovskaia provintsiia v semnadtsatom godu* (ed. Popova), p. 155;
Ina Rakitnikova, in *Delo Naroda*, no. 215 (November 21, 1917).

[32] Arepev. The authority of the family head is also emphasized in Ia.
Levanidov, "Podgotovka k izbiratelnoi kampanii v derevne," *Delo Naroda*,
no. 144 (September 2, 1917).

[33] *Ibid.*, no. 218 (November 24, 1917).

A total of three individualists [34] out of 642 voters makes the election look very bad indeed, until we remember that this must have been an extreme case, pulled out of the bag by the SR editors to point up their party's boast of being the "sovereign of the country's thoughts." Yet it was a stumbling block to any less pessimistic view of the election as long as there was nothing else to go on.

Finally, recourse was had to the provincial newspapers, rare and scattered though they be, and, after prolonged investigation, rescue came from the direction of Saratov. The excellent press of this "Athens of the Volga" printed a whole series of returns by villages for Saratov *uezd*, disclosing the nature of the rural vote in at least this one locality. A total of twenty-seven rural precincts form the basis of the study.[35] Three villages have been selected for presentation here, each being representative of a number of others and each being an authentic village — that is, not a settlement on the outskirts of Saratov city. The vote was divided as indicated in the tabulation on page 66.

It is quite obvious that the inhabitants of the first two villages moved as a mass without exercising their individual judgment, but it would be interesting to know why they moved in opposite directions. Perhaps in the one case there was some stimulus that did not prevail in the other, something that broke down the SR hegemony in Rybushka — if, as is likely, it once existed — but failed to shake it in Great Idolga.[36] We do not know. In any event a small minority stood out against the mass in both instances, daring to have a conviction of its own and daring to follow

[34] The 53 Tatars can not be considered as individualists since they were of a different race and religion — they belonged, in other words, to a different herd.

[35] A precinct does not necessarily coincide with a village. In many instances, however, this appears to have been the case — particularly in respect to larger villages (the usual type in Saratov province). The convenience of the voting public was the criterion, subject to administrative feasibility. See *Sputnik izbiratelia*, pp. 122–123.

[36] Both villages are given brief mention in *Rossiia: Polnoe geograficheskoe opisanie* (ed. Semenov), Vol. VI (1901), *Srednee i nizhnee Povolzhe i Zavolzhe*, pp. 482, 497.

	Great Idolga	Rybushka	Korsakovka
Registered	1,343	2,150	919
Voted	995*(74%)	1,638†(76%)	631 (69%)
List No:			
1 Kadet	8	0	2
2 SD Menshevik	0	0	1
3 Ukrainian and Tatar			
Bloc	0	25	0
4 Old Believer	0	0	86
5 Orthodox	3	12	3
6 Landowner	23	0	82
7 German	22	8	0
8 Popular Socialist ...	3	5	6
9 Faith and Order			
(rightist)	0	4	1
10 SD Bolshevik	64	1,516	127
11 Mordvin	0	0	0
12 SR	873	62	323

* Announced total. Total by parties one vote more.
† Announced total. Total by parties six votes less.

through. It is not large enough, however, to prevent the stock of the election from falling in the face of such returns. Then we turn to Korsakovka,[37] and the stock rises again. Here a real election was held. Here was no bovine stampede in one direction but rather a true diversity of opinion, reflected in a substantial vote for three other lists besides the leading one and in a sprinkling of votes over the rest of the field. Of the other twenty-four villages reported, ten were more or less like Great Idolga, three like Rybushka, and eleven like Korsakovka. In other words, fifteen villages gave an undue concentration [38] of votes to one party (eleven to the SR's and four to the Bolsheviks), twelve showed

[37] A village of Viazovka canton about 25 miles in a straight line north northwest of Saratov. Not mentioned in *ibid.* and can be located only on the most detailed maps in possession of the Hoover Library.

[38] This means two-thirds or more of the total vote. In order to deal with borderline cases, it is necessary to set an arbitrary standard. Only four precincts fall within the range 60–68 per cent.

a reasonable distribution among the parties,[39] and not a single one turned in a unanimous vote. That was the story for Saratov *uezd*, insofar as we have it.[40]

The returns presented, of course, are all from a district with a large urban center, the influence of which undoubtedly tended to radiate into the surrounding countryside, even though no extreme effect is noticeable in this instance. The villages cited were real ones. They were situated on fertile *chernozëm* and were highly productive, both in crops and in children, so that they were densely populated; since there was no lack of large estates to whet the greed — or revolutionary ardor — of the inhabitants, it was only natural that they should have favored either the SR's or the Bolsheviks.[41] Hence the returns are wholly admissible and may be used without hesitation.

Nevertheless, election figures for some locality remote from any suggestion of urban influence would be welcome, and it is possible to provide them in the case of three villages or precincts located in the same province but in a different *uezd*, the *uezd* of Khvalynsk, which occupies the northeastern corner of Saratov province and lies about halfway between Samara and Saratov, at a gratifying distance from both. Long a stronghold of the Old Believers because of its remote and secluded character, and having also its complement of sectarians, not excluding the orgiastic Khlysty and the dreadful Skoptsy, Khvalynsk *uezd* represents the backwoods of Russia in their most primitive form.[42] As a consequence, the returns in the accompanying table from Federovka village

---

[39] The leading party had less than half the vote in four of these, just over half in five others, and between 60–66 per cent in the remaining three.

[40] *Saratovskii Listok*, no. 247 (November 21, 1917), combined with *Saratovskii Vestnik*, no. 250 (November 21, 1917).

[41] Facts from *Rossiia: Polnoe geograficheskoe opisanie*, VI, 497–498.

[42] *Ibid.*, p. 460; N. Andreev, *Illiustrirovannyi putevoditel po Volge i eia pritokam Oke i Kame* (2nd ed.; Moscow, n.d.), pp. 240–241; A. Lepeshinskaia and B. Dobrynin, *Volga* (Moscow, 1911), pp. 176–181, where Khvalynsk is called the Old Believers' Palestine. The Old Believers rank as schismatics, not as sectarians. The Khlysty were flagellants; the Skoptsy sought purification through self-mutilation, especially of the sexual organs.

and from two other precincts in Federovka canton are highly to be prized.[43]

	Federovka Village	Vorobievski Precinct	Ershovski Precinct
Registered	1,290	not given	not given
Voted	847 *	not given	not given
List No:			
1 Kadet	46	0	4
2 SD Menshevik	0	0	0
3 Ukrainian and Tatar Bloc	0	0	0
4 Old Believer	92	8	456
5 Orthodox	16	3	13
6 Landowner	83	77	4
7 German	0	0	1
8 Popular Socialist . . .	29	0	0
9 Faith and Order (rightist)	53	4	1
10 SD Bolshevik	58	1	46
11 Mordvin	0	0	0
12 SR	467	35	105

* Total by parties 844. Two votes were disallowed — one unaccounted for.

It is obvious that Ershovski and Vorobievski precincts are exceptional as far as voting preference is concerned; there were relatively few villages in the Russia of 1917 where the Old Believers would predominate (in the political sense), and fewer still where the hated landowners would come out on top. Only Federovka can qualify as representative in this sense, though even there the Bolshevik vote is abnormally low. But that is beside the point. The thing to note here is that in these backwoods there was no unanimity of sentiment nor even an approach to it. True, there is evidence of a mass reaction in the large vote compiled by a single favored list in each instance, but there were

[43] *Saratovskii Vestnik*, no. 251 (November 23, 1917). Federovka was a larger village (*selo*) located on a high bluff overlooking the Volga, into which it always seemed on the verge of sliding. Vorobievski and Ershovski possibly were lesser villages (*derevni*); they could not be located on map.

plenty of strays from the herd in all three villages. In Federovka a very large minority rejected the SR list and further affirmed its independence by splitting up its vote among seven parties. This was an unusually satisfactory dispersion of strength. And even in Ershovski precinct, where Old Ritualism retained something of its pristine vigor, twenty-three hold-outs preferred some other conservative list, and 151 votes were cast for the Revolution. Rural Russia, as reflected in these figures, does not look so bad as might have been expected.

In the entire province of Saratov, minus Kamyshin *uezd*, the SR's received 564,250 votes and the Bolsheviks 225,000.[44] Enough has been said to show the reader that, unfortunately, these totals were not amassed in any such healthy fashion as a 5:2 division in the average village, but rather in large part by a top-heavy vote for the Bolsheviks in many villages, overbalanced by an equally top-heavy vote for the SR's in a much greater number of villages. Yet it must be remembered, also, that to a considerable extent the totals were amassed in thoroughly legitimate fashion by the inclusion of returns from a large number of settlements like Korsakovka,[45] where there had been a real division of opinion and, consequently, a real election.

[44] See Chapter II, note 4. The other ten lists drew 165,309 votes.
[45] Here, incidentally, the ratio between the leading parties was 323:127 or almost exactly 5:2.

CHAPTER VI

CONCLUSION

As we come to our conclusion, then, the image before us in respect to the validity of this election is neither all black nor all white; it is rather a somber gray. The village vote is indubitably the Achilles' heel of the election. In the towns the vote was along class lines and there is every indication that it was a fairly conscious one, the only defect being an indifferent turnout at the polls. But in the villages an inferior political consciousness permitted the populace to be swayed now one way and now the other, depending upon the intensity and the persistence of the pressure applied. Apparently in numberless cases there was a herd, and it did stampede. Yet in extenuation of the showing of the village, it may be urged that a considerable element stood out from the herd and exhibited a will of its own. How large a proportion it was cannot be estimated, in view of the paucity of information. But we know that the Bolsheviks experienced a bitter disappointment in respect to the Ural industrial region, where the working class stood firmly behind its vanguard, was strong in numbers and militant in spirit, and yet failed to swing the village behind it, going down in overwhelming defeat before the SR's by a margin of 664,883 to 267,577.[1] "The Urals," commissar Uritski told his party's Petrograd committee, "have not justified our expectations." [2] This is by all odds the most resounding failure to coerce or cajole peasants of which we have record.

But even in those cases where they succumbed to pressure, it

[1] Interview with the SR deputy, Tarabukin, in *Delo Naroda*, no. 242 (December 28, 1917). The Bolsheviks had counted on ten deputies but got only four (election figures for Perm province from Sviatitski's table). Remoteness from the front may well have been a factor; soldiers, for the most part peasants themselves, excelled workers as vote-getters.

[2] Trotski, *Sochineniia*, III, Part II, 364, quoted in Vishniak, *Vserossiiskoe Uchreditelnoe Sobranie*, p. 90.

must be borne in mind that the only question was whether they would be brought over to the Bolsheviks or held in line by the SR's. Never do we hear of their being won over, say, by the Kadets. Indeed, in those rare instances where the Kadets had influence with the peasants it required only a modicum of agitation to destroy that party's prestige and swing them over to the Bolsheviks or SR's.[3] The conservative press sorrowfully acknowledged that "the village gives but few votes to the party of Popular Freedom,"[4] although a prominent economist had warned its readers months before the election that their complacency was due for a rude awakening if they continued to regard peasant support of the PSR as the momentary infatuation of a class innately conservative in point of view. The peasantry in truth had little understanding of the SR program, he wrote, and it did have its own views, but those views in some ways were even more radical than the party's, for the mass was quite plainly getting ready to expropriate not only the squires (*pomeshchiki*) but also the well-to-do peasants themselves.[5] The village was unquestionably in a revolutionary frame of mind as it prepared to vote, wholly unwilling to listen to conservative arguments and uncertain only about the brand of radicalism it would take. Between radicalism and conservatism it never wavered.

Thus the malleability of the peasant will had definite limits. It

[3] *Derevenskaia Bednota*, no. 38 (November 25, 1917). The incident cited occurred in Glubokovski canton, Opochetsk *uezd*, Pskov province.

[4] *Russkoe Slovo*, no. 259 (November 26, 1917).

[5] Tugan-Baranovski, "Derevnia i Uchreditelnoe Sobranie," *ibid.*, no. 163 (July 19, 1917). Durnovo in 1914 had prophesied the triumph of extremism in the event of war and revolution; because of the nature of the Russian people, things would never stop with a political revolution. "A particularly fertile field for social upheavals is, of course, offered by Russia, where the mass of the people undoubtedly embraces the principles of an unconscious socialism . . . a political revolution in Russia is impossible, and every revolutionary movement will inevitably degenerate into a socialistic one . . . The Russian common man, peasant and worker alike, does not seek political rights, which are not necessary to him, and not understandable" ("Zapiska," *Krasnaia Nov*, no. 6/10 [November–December 1922], pp. 195–196). One can only marvel at Durnovo's depth of comprehension as well as at the accuracy of his predictions.

could be beaten out on the anvil, but not on any anvil. And it is very easy to explain why the Bolshevik smith could often hammer it to better avail than his SR rival. A large and growing element within the PSR was becoming less and less distinguishable from Bolshevism; right after the election it would split off from the parent body and become the Party of the Left SR's.[6] Then there was the influence of Lenin's barefaced appropriation, without changing so much as a word, of the SR land program, and its promulgation as one of the first decrees of his new regime.[7] The effect can be judged from the words of an SR delegate who was explaining to a peasants' congress the surprise victory of the Bolsheviks in Moscow province: "Drunk with the destruction of Moscow, the Bolshevik garrison scattered over the countryside with Lenin's decrees in its hands and slander on its lips." [8] The Bolsheviks were promising the moon to the peasants at this time, outbidding the SR's in every particular, so that it was only natural that the simple people, ignorant of the essence of the Marxist program, should have fallen an easy prey to demagogues who carefully concealed what lay in store for them during the period

[6] The election, therefore, does not measure the strength of this element. The lists of party candidates were drawn up long before the schism occurred; they were top-heavy with older party workers whose radicalism had abated by 1917. The people voted indiscriminately for the SR label (the whole electoral process was attuned to voting by party lists instead of by individual candidates), giving only a handful of votes to SR splinter lists, whether of the left or right, in the few districts where such were offered. But inasmuch as the left-wing element controlled the party organization in some districts, it rigged the lists accordingly and mustered about forty deputies in the Constituent Assembly after the schism in late November. That is not a fair measure of its strength, however, for the leftward current was doubtlessly stronger everywhere on November 12 than when the lists had been drawn up. This whole question of the correlation of party factionalism with candidates' lists is a very complex one and cannot be treated in a study of this scope. The writer's judgments are based on his unpublished dissertation, "The Party of the Socialist-Revolutionaries and the Russian Revolution of 1917" (Harvard University, 1939).

[7] *Sobranie uzakonenii i rasporiazhenii rabochego i krestianskogo pravitelstva* (2nd ed.; Moscow, n.d.), section I, no. 1 (December 1, 1917), article 3, pp. 3–5; Lenin, "Vybory v Uchreditelnoe Sobranie i diktatura proletariata," *Sochineniia* (2nd ed.), XXIV, 640–641, and 828, n. 200.

[8] *Delo Naroda*, no. 231 (December 13, 1917).

of militant communism and the era of the Five Year Plans. Bolshevism could never have triumphed in Russia had it not been able to play upon the peasants' confused but revolutionary consciousness.

Besides the political immaturity of so large a portion of the voting public, the election may be indicted on the ground that it came off during a paroxysm of revolution and hence captured a mood that was inflamed and evanescent. In truth, each of the major parties received a substantial vote which might have gone away from it in normal times and certainly could not have been relied upon in any future test of strength. Thus the avalanche of votes for the PSR was not so much an expression of party allegiance as of the demand for expropriation without compensation; *after* the peasants had the land in their possession, they might have developed a taste for property and hence might have gravitated in the direction of some more conservative grouping. The most remarkable paradox of the election was the preponderance of rural votes in the Bolshevik column, and this was due, almost certainly, not to the consciousness of the village pauperdom — which the Bolsheviks would have claimed as their own — but to the influence of the front, either directly in the form of soldiers' votes or indirectly in the form of those of their wives and neighbors at home. The fierce agitation of peasants in uniform among those who had stayed at home flooded the urns with Bolshevik ballots. Yet this factor of war weariness, potent as it was, could only have been a transitory phenomenon: the army was in full state of distintegration and after the process had run its course and peace had been established, the village and the ex-soldiers themselves would have turned their thoughts to other matters. As for the Kadets, their middle-class and intellectual constituency had been reinforced by a rightist element which under other conditions would no doubt have gone its own way.[9] Even the Menshevik

[9] "Za neimeniem luchshego podavaite golos za spisok partii narodnoi svobody No. 1" ("For want of something better, give your vote to List No. 1, the Party of Popular Freedom"), ran the exhortation in *Fonar*, no. 10 (November 20, 1917), a newspaper published in Moscow under a

vote was not solid in that nearly half of it came from Georgia, where nationalism had long masqueraded in Menshevik trappings and where it was now about ready to doff the disguise.

But each party had granite as well as chalk in its make-up. Many peasants would have remembered the PSR as the party that gave them the land, and a tradition of support would have been built up such as is necessary to the political life of a republic; perhaps the party would have adjusted its program to the changing psychology of many of its supporters and would have retained not merely a part but nearly all of its following. The Bolshevik party had already conquered the Russian proletariat by November of 1917, acquiring a solid core around which to amass a miscellaneous following from other social groups. And the Kadets, as the standard-bearers of capitalism and Western liberalism, likewise rested on a firm though circumscribed base. Thus a free election held a few years later no doubt would have revealed a very considerable redistribution of strength without, however, reducing any of the major parties to a negligible quantity.

These two indictments of the election to the All-Russian Constituent Assembly — on grounds of abnormal timing and a prevailingly low level of political consciousness — are both serious; neither is damning. And the indictment on grounds of distortion through fraud and violence must be disallowed. The vote in question, therefore, stands on middle ground between normal elections in Western countries and the manipulated elections which have become so prominent a feature of our own day — in open form in totalitarian countries and, in other Western countries, in the restriction of the voters' choice to candidates with a similar point of view, as in the presidential election of 1940, for instance.

The significance of the election in history is, of course, bound up with the Constituent Assembly to which it gave birth. As a

---

masthead which proclaimed it to be a "patriotic paper but not at all counter-revolutionary." It was, however, beyond dispute a rightist organ, for its tone was monarchistic and it favored a limited suffrage, under which only the elite could vote. See the editorial in this issue by P. K[ochmanski]; also his article, "Za kogo sleduet podat golos na vyborakh."

political phenomenon the assembly may be considered from two opposing points of view. Either it was a victim of circumstances, a noble experiment incorporating a sound principle but doomed by the crisis into which it was born, or else it was an attempt to transplant an alien concept of government to soil where it could never flourish. Certainly the Eurasian climate has not been propitious to the growth of self-governing institutions; not free communities, but vast empires, responsive to a single will and organized on the basis of military service above and slave labor below, have been the order of the day. And this regardless of the epoch of history, the human material involved, or the ideological window-dressing provided. All we can say is that the weight of the past did not determine the results of this election; on the one occasion when they have been free to make a choice, the Russian people voted in favor of self-government. Perhaps they would not have done so the next time; perhaps the grave was ready for the experiment before it was conceived — we do not know.

The political significance of the Constituent Assembly, therefore, cannot be determined, at least not at present. But its position in history is secure. History records the failures as well as the successes of mankind — rather more the failures, one is tempted to say, than the successes — and the All-Russian Constituent Assembly, together with the election which produced it, will always be an arresting episode in the destiny of a great people, whether it marks the course to which that people will some day return, or whether it remains a lonely monument to a principle that could never germinate on the plain of Eastern Europe.

APPENDIX

To PRESENT the results of an election held in a vast, multinational empire amid the chaotic conditions that prevailed in 1917 is an intricate task. The table that follows is complex enough but many details have been suppressed. Naturally, in the work of simplification some information has had to be sacrificed. The returns have been compiled from a wide variety of sources. They are as complete and accurate as careful and long-continued research can make them. Nevertheless, numerous imperfections remain. Complete and official returns are the exception rather than the rule. For many districts the figures are known to be incomplete; for many others there is no indication in the sources as to the degree of completeness. In some cases only round figures are given; in others, the vote for certain parties is omitted. Sometimes a major portion of the vote may be announced as a lump sum without being differentiated by parties, even though one or more of the parties thus cavalierly disposed of may enjoy great local strength. And, finally, for certain districts there are no returns whatever. No claim can be made, therefore, that this is a definitive compilation. Yet it has value as the fullest and most accurate set of returns in existence.

ELECTION RETURNS BY DISTRICTS

Region and District	PSR [a]	SD Bolshevik	SD Menshevik	Minor Socialist Parties	Constitutional Democrat	Other Non-socialist Parties	Ukrainian Parties	Mohammedan Parties	Other Nationality Parties	Unclassified	Total Vote
Northern											
1. Archangel ‡ b	85,272	21,779	7,335	....	12,086	....	....	....	....	1,160	127,632
2. Olonets * b	127,062	....	126,827	....	....	....	....	....	....	....	127,062
3. Vologda ‡	320,528	67,650	....	8,071	22,912	....	....	....	....	3,742	422,903
Northwestern—Lake											
4. Petrograd Prov.	119,761	229,698	5,700	9,900	64,859	4,491	....	....	....	28,209	462,618
5. Pskov	269,267	139,690	1,952	2,440	19,026	1,828	....	....	....	6,914	441,117
6. Novgorod*	220,665	203,658	9,336	12,297	31,480	8,982	....	....	....	....	486,418
Baltic											
7. Esthonia	3,200	119,863	....	....	....	....	....	....	176,781	....	299,844
8. Livonia †	....	97,781	7,046	....	....	....	....	....	31,253	....	136,080
Western—White Russian											
9. Vitebsk *	150,279	287,101	12,471	3,599	8,132	16,602	....	....	82,354	....	560,538•
10. Minsk †	181,673	579,087	16,277	....	10,724	13,505	....	....	115,980 d	....	917,246
11. Smolensk *	250,134	361,062	7,901	2,210	29,274	5,300	....	....	1,708	645	658,234•
12. Mogilev (no returns)	....	....	....	....	....	....	....	....	....	....	....
Central											
13. Tver †	186,030	362,687	22,552	2,338	32,830	....	....	....	....	9,412	606,437
14. Iaroslavl	216,744	131,124	18,240	5,014	59,400	....	....	....	....	....	439,934
15. Kostroma	248,951	223,353	19,529	....	41,242	17,915	....	....	....	....	550,990
16. Vladimir *	197,311	337,941	13,074	8,390	38,035	9,209	....	....	....	....	603,960
17. Moscow Prov.‡	153,458	337,492	26,877	12,586	42,415	24,546	....	....	....	....	597,374
18. Tula ‡	216,265	219,297	9,605	1,802	21,478	8,773	....	....	....	9,138	477,585
19. Riazañ ‡	397,229	251,815	4,389	5,216	27,808	8,773	....	....	....	....	695,230•
20. Nizhni Novgorod *	314,003	133,950	7,634	2,666	34,726	64,658	....	....	....	22,260	579,897
21. Kaluga (no returns)	....	....	....	....	....	....	....	....	....	....	....
Central Black-Earth											
22. Orël †	305,013	144,492	8,824	....	13,477	8,656	....	....	....	8,330	480,136
23. Kursk *	868,743	119,127	6,037	8,594	47,199	8,027	....	....	....	....	1,058,356
24. Voronezh *	875,300	151,517	8,658	6,116	36,488	....	11,871 e	....	....	....	1,097,977
25. Tambov *	835,556	240,052	22,425	7,408	47,548	(12,460)	....	6,222	....	920	1,173,191
26. Penza *	517,226	54,731	4,726	4,336	25,407	....	....	29,821	....	....	636,247

	1	2	3	4	5	6	7	8	9	10	11
Southeastern—Volga											
27. Samara *	690,341	195,132	5,181	5,313	44,507	23,263	5,240	126,816	112,017f	....	1,207,810
28. Simbirsk	345,200	70,335	3,681	45,000	16,718	....	....	57,000	9,094	....	537,934
29. Saratov ‡	564,250	225,000	(11,308)	(4,666)	(20,120)	(15,211)	53,000g	....	....	51,970	954,559
30. Astrakhan †	100,482	36,023	(2,220)	....	13,017	16,400oh	....	25,023	....	942	194,107
Black Sea–North Caucasus											
31. Don *	478,901	205,497	(6,327)	(2,620)	43,345	640,000h	....	....	....	29,930	1,406,620
32. Taurida †	300,150	(15,642)	(11,118)	....	(29,904)	....	61,559	60,858	....	45,519	524,750
33. Stavropol *	291,395	17,430	....	....	10,898	....	....	....	....	8,193	327,916
34. Kuban (no election)	....	....	....	....	....	....	....	....	....	....	....
35. Terek-Daghestan (no election)	....	....	....	....	....	....	....	....	....	....	....
36. Caspian (no returns)	....	....	....	....	....	....	....	....	....	....	....
Kama–Ural											
37. Kazan *	260,000	50,000	4,906	12,993	32,000	14,000	....	253,151	226,496	5,050	858,596
38. Viatka ‡	300,503	78,278	11,757	26,253	22,404	8,016	....	37,781	....	....	484,992
39. Perm	664,883	267,577	27,439	28,964	111,252	47,600	....	....	....	127,963	1,275,678
40. Ufa	322,276	48,135	2,334	11,442	15,653	....	....	305,121	....	259,274	904,235
41. Orenburg *	110,172	163,425	....	....	24,757	....	....	....	....	378,511i	676,865
Siberia											
42. Tobolsk *	388,328	....	12,061	54,513	13,793	....	....	25,830	....	....	494,525
43. Altai	621,377	45,286	3,785	6,068	12,108	17,292	....	....	8,048	....	713,964
44. Tomsk	541,153	51,456	5,769	18,488	18,618	....	....	....	....	....	635,484
45. Ienisei †	229,671	96,618	4,581	11,674	12,263	2,452	....	....	....	....	356,779e
46. Irkutsk	113,378	31,587	5,534	(6,925)	8,834	(2,653)	....	....	(15,464)	30,098	214,473
47. Transbaikal †	104,220	17,260	4,500	....	7,200	....	....	....	....	37,622	170,802e
48. Amur †	96,658	32,255	12,000	....	14,649	....	....	....	....	24,600	180,162
49. Iakutsk (no returns)	....	....	....	....	....	....	....	....	....	....	....
50. Kamchatka (no returns)	....	....	....	....	....	....	....	....	....	....	....
51. Chinese East. R.R. (no returns)	....	....	....	....	....	....	....	....	....	....	....
Ukraine											
52. Podolia ‡	10,170	27,540	4,028	852	7,951	284	656,116	....	123,319j	....	830,260
53. Volhynia	27,575	35,612	16,947	....	22,397	....	569,044	....	55,967k	76,666	804,208
54. Kiev	19,201	59,413	11,532	....	28,630	48,641	1,256,271	....	(153,276)l	50,763	1,627,727
55. Chernigov	105,565	271,174	10,813	10,089	28,864	30,658	484,456	....	31,116	911	973,646
56. Poltava *	198,437m	64,400	5,993	4,391	18,105	61,115	760,022	....	34,631	2,102	1,149,256
57. Kharkov	650,386m	110,846	17,775	48,983	59,509	28,013	(see PSR)	....	13,014	....	928,526
58. Ekaterinoslav*	231,717	213,163	26,909	16,859	27,551	34,665	556,012	....	86,173n	....	1,193,049
59. Kherson ‡	354,312m	77,112	14,936	....	54,493	....	72,504	....	(43,608)	77,416	694,391
60. Bessarabia (no returns)	....	....	....	....	....	....	....	....	....	....	....
Transcaucasia											
61. Transcaucasia *	105,265	86,935	569,362	....	24,551	....	....	....	(350,000)o	751,340	1,887,453

ELECTION RETURNS BY DISTRICTS (continued)

Region and District	PSR [a]	SD Bolshevik	SD Menshevik	Minor Socialist Parties	Constitutional Democrat	Other Nonsocialist Parties	Ukrainian Parties	Mohammedan Parties	Other Nationality Parties	Unclassified	Total Vote
Metropolitan											
62. Petrograd *	152,230	424,027	29,167	30,728	246,506	55,456	4,219p	....	....	....	942,333
63. Moscow *	62,260	366,148	21,597	37,813	263,859	8,664	....	....	4,422	....	764,763
Army											
64. Northern Front *	249,832	471,828	10,420	5,868	13,687	....	88,956	....	....	8,069	849,591
65. Western Front *	180,582	653,430	8,000	(2,429)	16,750	(3,055)	85,062	(15,133)	(3,510)	....	976,000
66. SW Front	402,930	300,112	79,630	....	13,724	....	168,354	....	....	42,673	1,007,423
67. Roumanian Front	679,471	167,000	33,858	....	21,438	....	180,576	....	....	46,257	1,128,600
68. Caucasus Front (no returns)	....	....	....	....	....	....	....	....	....	....	....
Fleet											
69. Black Sea *	22,251	10,771	1,943	....	....	....	12,895	....	....	4,769	52,629
70. Baltic b	15,947	43,053	....	9,736	....	28	....	....	....	....	68,764
Central Asia											
71–80. Ten districts (no election)	....	....	....	....	....	....	....	....	....	....	....
Totals q	15,848,004	9,844,637	1,364,826	505,590	1,986,601	1,262,418	4,957,067	942,736	1,678,231	2,151,368	41,686,876r

Figures in parentheses taken from earlier, less complete tabulation.

* Known to be complete.

† Known to be only slightly incomplete.

‡ Known to be substantially incomplete (one *uezd* or more missing).

a Official lists only. Dissident SR lists included under "minor socialist."

b Different voting system: balloting for individual candidates instead of for lists. Vote taken is for highest candidate of each party. On Olonets, see note g to table on page 17.

c Corrected total; slight deviation from announced total. On Transbaikal, see Chapter II, note 7.

d Jewish Nationalist, 65,046; Jewish socialist, 11,064; Polish Nationalist, 36,882; White Russian, 2,988.

e Joint list: Ukrainian SR, Left SR, and Polish Socialist Party (PPS)

f German Nationalist, 47,705; German Socialist, 42,156; Bashkir Federalist, 13,100; Chuvash, 9,056.

g Joint list, Ukrainian and Tatar.

h Cossack vote. On Don Region, see Chapter II, note 8.

i See Chapter II, note 12.

j Jewish Nationalist, 62,547; other Jewish, 13,860; Polish, 46,912.

k Two Jewish lists.

l Jewish Nationalist, 86,943; Jewish socialist, 35,443; Polish, 30,890.

m Joint list, Ukrainian SR and SR.

n Jewish Nationalist, 37,032; Jewish socialist, 14,021; German, 25,977; Greek, 9,143.

o Armenian Dashnaktsutiun. See Chapter II, note 18.

p Joint list, Ukrainian socialist bloc and Jewish Socialist Workers' Party.

q Exclusive of joint lists herein indicated.

r Total by districts and also corrected total by parties (represents addition of joint lists herein indicated to foregoing totals by parties, but with deduction of 126,827 from Menshevik column to eliminate overlapping with SR vote in Olonets district).

BIBLIOGRAPHICAL NOTE

THE literature on the Constituent Assembly is not extensive and for the most part concerns the history of that body rather than the election which produced it. The three studies made of the election itself — those of Sviatitski, Lenin, and the Archives of the October Revolution — have been mentioned in the text (see pp. 4–5).

It had been the official intent to publish information pertaining to the election in the bulletins of the All-Russian Electoral Commission (*Izvestiia Vserossiiskoi po delam o vyborakh v Uchreditelnoe Sobranie Komissii*). But since this organ was a creation of the Provisional Government, it came into conflict with the Soviet authority after the October Revolution, its work was seriously hampered, and eventually it was suppressed. Preparations for the election as well as the opening phase of the controversy are described in the bulletins, and beginning with No. 24 (December 16, 1917), returns were published by districts. Unfortunately for the student of history, however, this most important of statistical sources is abruptly terminated with the next issue (December 20, 1917), leaving a valuable but fragmentary record of the reports from district commissions. The last two numbers containing returns are exceedingly rare and it is doubtful that even Sviatitski saw them.

The cessation of official reports and the incompleteness of the statistical data presented by Sviatitski and the Soviet Archives throw the investigator back upon the only two remaining sources of information: the press and local accounts of the revolution. Although provincial studies began to be published early in the Soviet period, most of them appeared about 1927–28 in connection with the tenth anniversary of the October Revolution. Uneven in quality and not infrequently marked by a low level of performance, these accounts nevertheless reward the student who has the time and patience to go through them; the better ones shed a good deal of light on the election campaign in the province under consideration and may even present a tabulation of returns. It is to be regretted that for some provinces the events of 1917 have never been written up.

As for the press, the search for election data is not unlike looking for a needle in a haystack. The more obvious reports are likely to have been worked over by Sviatitski, though not necessarily so — nothing can be taken for granted when one is dealing with the election to the All-Russian Constituent Assembly. The Soviet press is not as helpful as it could have been, considering the vantage ground which it occupied: as opinion in government circles became increasingly hostile to the Constituent Assembly, less and less space was devoted to the election in the columns of Bolshevik newspapers and a campaign of depreciation set in. This is particularly true of *Pravda*; as for the *Izvestiia Tsentralnago Ispolnitelnago Komiteta i petrogradskago soveta*, its coverage of the election is uniformly disappointing, in the beginning as at the end.

The opposition press, especially the nonsocialist press, labored under the disability of being hounded by the new regime just at the time that returns were coming in. Thus the newspaper which published more detailed information than any other, the *Russkoe Slovo* of Moscow, was suppressed outright at the end of November. The *Russkiia Vedomosti* of the same city managed to keep going during the whole period of voting; its observations on the election are the most trustworthy of all, but statistically it leaves something to be desired. The best treatment of the election in a socialist newspaper, with respect both to figures and comment, is to be found in the Petrograd *Delo Naroda*, the central organ of the PSR. Other metropolitan newspapers yield less information than those mentioned, but there is always the chance that some item was included in one paper which did not appear in the others.

There is no doubt that a study of the election would be enriched by a systematic survey of the provincial press, but the materials are so dispersed and inaccessible that they virtually defy inspection. Even where it has been possible to consult the files of a local newspaper, the value of the investigation has been lessened by missing numbers. Enough was found, however, to indicate the fruitfulness of this source if the obstacles to its exploitation could be overcome.

There is also no doubt that the central archives could be made to yield more than they have thus far at the hands of Soviet scholars. But in view of the ravages of war and revolution and the lapse of time, it seems unlikely that the complete record of the election can be assembled, even under more favorable circumstances than hitherto have prevailed.

PART TWO

The Election Revisited

CHAPTER VII

THE SETTING AND THE ROLE OF
THE PROVISIONAL GOVERNMENT

ONCE, AND ONLY ONCE, in their history have the Russian and associated peoples experienced an election without constraints, when suffrage was universal and voting direct, equal, and secret, with a minimum of violence. In the tsarist period, during the short period when elections were held, the franchise was limited and the voting was in stages and unequal; it was also subject to intimidation, or at least pressure, except in 1906, when Count Witte had permitted a free election (he had an upper house and a largely intact officers' corps to fall back on). In the Soviet period, apart from a certain number of dummy nonpartisans, the choice has been limited to a single party. Only in 1989 has the choice widened enough to give meaning to an election, and only in 1989 has the intent at the top been to countenance free voting; yet in the mixed system now in effect numerous features remain that contravene the ultra-democratic, four-fold formula, and it is too early to judge what happened down below, in the sticks of Russia and in outlying lands. Nevertheless, a change for the better has taken place—in the eighth decade of the new order.

It was otherwise in the morning of revolution, during the period of liberty between the crash of monarchy and the onset of communism. The election of delegates to a constituent assembly, beginning in November of 1917 and extending over a period of weeks before trailing off into 1918—technically it was never completed—could not have rested on a broader franchise nor could provisions for access to the ballot have been more generous. The many parties and groups and their adherence to principle guaranteed to every citizen a means of expressing his or her views; the conduct of the election was prevailingly free, despite sporadic violence; and votes were counted as cast. Not only the crasser means of disfiguring the popular will but the more devious ones—choking off access to the ballot, in the case of newly established or smaller parties, and tampering with the results to produce fraudulent returns—were not practiced on this occasion.

Only a few attempts have been made to reconstruct this unique phenomenon in Russian history. The first was by the Socialist Revolutionary statistician N. V. Sviatitski in 1918 (*Itogi vyborov vo vserossiiskoe Uchreditel'noe Sobranie* [Moscow: Zemlia i Volia, 1918]). Unrivaled in his knowledge of the subject but hampered by the chaotic conditions of the time, he managed to put together a total of 36,257,960 votes in 54 of the 80 electoral districts. Not all of his figures are correct and many are missing, yet his work remains to this day the point of departure for any investigation of the subject. It was the basis for Lenin's analysis of the election, the Soviet leader being content to take over Sviatitski's statistical findings without change or addition—a great pity, because he had the authority, if he had chosen to use it, to produce the complete and official returns for at least the central provinces of Russia, where his party did well. The opportunity was lost, in all probability never to return.

The second attempt—in the statistical sense—was made under the auspices of the Archives of the October Revolution (*Vserossiiskoe Uchreditel'noe Sobranie* [Moscow and Leningrad: State Publishing Firm, 1930], prepared for printing by I. S. Malchevski). What happened is best described by those in charge:

> In preparing the present book for publication, the staff had in mind to give the numerical results of the election to the Constituent Assembly but had to abandon this plan because, on inspection of the materials in the statistical section of the Archives of the October Revolution, it appeared that the statistical information sent in to the All-Russian Electoral Commission, without being worked over, was scattered and incomplete and did not admit of the possibility of presenting a more or less definitive account of the election for the country as a whole. Inquiries from the Central Archives as to producing the desired materials in the provinces yielded no positive results.

Before abandoning the effort to assemble the numerical results and concentrating on drawing up a list of members that produced 715 names out of a possible 815—a notable achievement—the editors did succeed in adding four more electoral districts with 4,298,854 votes to Sviatitski's tabulation. The worth of their contribution is lessened, however, by their reporting of only the SR, SD Bolshevik, and Constitutional Democratic totals and their suppression of even the mention of competing lists that may have been secondary from a general point of view but were of primary significance in their own areas (Cossack lists on the Don and in Orenburg province, Bashkir in Orenburg, Tatar and Armenian in the Transcaucasus). As a result, the bulk of the vote in the four districts reposes in an undivided residue and the investigator is left with a feeling of having been cheated.

Several lessons may be learned from this aborted enterprise. The failure of a quasi-official effort, presumably with every advantage at its command, bears witness to the difficulty of the task. The central archives are revealed to be in an unsatisfactory state, in respect alike to what they contain and to what they do not contain. A great part of the statistical material was never sent in, imparting a spotty character to what was received, itself in raw condition and replete with lacunae. Appeals for assistance to the provinces fell on deaf ears. Only coercive measures could have overcome the sloth and bovine indifference of the provincial authorities; the Soviet regime, we may assume, did not care to exert pressure to compile a record of what had been one of its most signal defeats.

Despite the discouraging or even forbidding precedent, the fascination of the topic led me to undertake a third attempt, which took form as the work that appeared first in 1950 and that constitutes Part One of this volume. Besides presenting my own analysis, it comprised returns from 60 of the 80 districts with a total of 41,686,876 votes. The work is more substantial than it seems because of the necessity of taking away from, as well as adding to, what went before: thus the elimination of Mogilev province and the Caucasian Front from Sviatitski's count as representing nothing more than a crude estimate lops off a million and a quarter votes, nor is this the only reduction. Even so, one-fourth of the districts are missing and a good many of the 60 included are incomplete. Still plenty of room for improvement here.

Into this situation eighteen years later came the Soviet historian L. M. Spirin with an ambitious compilation that had pretensions of being definitive (*Klassy i partii v grazhdanskoi voine v Rossii, 1917–1920* gg. [Moscow: Mysl', 1968]). He produced figures for 65 of 78 (sic) electoral districts and amassed 44,433,309 votes. At first glance it seemed unlikely that much could be done beyond what he had accomplished, but an inspection of his tabulation soon revealed to the practiced eye errors and gaps and shortcomings that left room enough for further investigation.

And so beginning in 1976 I set earnestly to work to revise the study published a quarter of a century before. On the positive side, there had been a great outpouring of literature in the years since 1950, particularly in connection with the fortieth anniversary of the October Revolution in 1957 and the fiftieth in 1967, but also to a lesser extent during the years between and beyond. Much of this literature purported to examine October in the provinces, precisely the sort of investigation that should have proved valuable to a reconstruction of the election. On the negative side, the advantage enjoyed by Spirin in the form of access to the central archives continued to be denied to an outsider, above all to an independent outsider. Yet this handicap was not an insuperable obstacle, for the story of the election of 1917 will never be told from what reposes in the central archives. It would be helped by such an inspection, nothing more. The present study, the fifth attempt to record what happened, has at least something for 70 of the 80 electoral districts, yielding a total vote of 44,218,555.

A word about the difficulty of the subject, since it has been beastly hard to do even this much. At the start, of all eighty districts in this vast empire, exactly two could boast of returns that were both complete and official. To these Ukrainian provinces of Poltava and Ekaterinoslav I was able to add the Northern Front on the one occasion I was admitted to the Marx-Engels Institute. And that was all. It still is all. Things are not really that bad, however. Today a considerable number of districts may be presumed to be complete, and they would also be official if there were any agency to make them so. The most striking evidence of the degree of difficulty is, of course, the abandonment in 1930 by the central archival authorities of their hope of presenting returns for the whole country. Now, well over half a century later and more than seventy years after Sviatitski's virgin endeavor, that hope remains unfulfilled. As for the present endeavor, all I can claim, despite long-sustained effort and intimate knowledge of the subject, is that it has narrowed the distance to be traversed toward that goal—assuming that it can ever be attained.

What are the reasons for this inordinate difficulty? The usual ones, put forth in any account and given also in Part One, are the Bolshevik overthrow of the Provisional Government on the eve of the election; the ensuing conflict between the new authority and the All-Russian Electoral Commission created by the defunct one; the suppression of this commission by the Soviet government, entailing the disruption of the electoral machinery; and the encroachment of other concerns, seemingly more imperative and certainly more preemptive of public attention: the advance toward a separate peace, the decomposition of the army, provisioning uncertainties in the cities, peasant disorders in the countryside, the ferment of nationalities, and the preparations for civil war. All of these developments overshadowed the election and most likely would have defeated its purpose in any event. But concealed from view has been the truth that the body it would bring into being already had at best only a desperate chance for survival.

The responsibility for setting the Constituent Assembly on the road to ruin rests squarely on the shoulders of the Provisional

Government. It was a nonrevolutionary government that an un-
kind fate had conferred on a revolution destined to be unsur-
passed in breadth and in depth, and clearly foreshadowed as
such by the prelude of 1905–1907. Only its desire for a change at
the apex of the imperial structure to ensure more vigorous prosecution of the war interferes with its being termed counterrevolutionary. Too much has been made of its dedication to establishing a regime of political and personal liberty. Its real purpose was
to hold Russia in the war. Nothing was to detract from that
purpose, especially an election from which the pace-setting element in the government, the Constitutional Democratic party,
had only the worst to expect, knowing that it was shut out of the
villages and would be swamped by the peasant tide. If there had
to be an election, then not before the late fall, when military
operations would be at a minimum (as though there would be
any at all). Hence the procrastination of the Provisional Government. Precious weeks were wasted in sterile debates on such
subjects as electoral rights for the defunct dynasty, no member of
which could have mustered more than a corporal's guard (better,
a general's guard). At first there had been talk of holding the
election in August, but August yielded to September, September
yielded to October, and it required an ultimatum from Minister-
President Kerenski's own party to hold the government to a date
in November. Actually, November 25 marked merely the beginning of the electoral process, which dragged on into December
and then into January of 1918. It was a miserable performance.

Even worse were the technical preparations. The delay on the
part of a regime at heart unwilling to have an election but unable
to say so was at length overcome, but the stinting of the election
in funds, in materials, and above all in personnel never could be
made good. Innumerable are the complaints about the shortage
of money, printer's ink, and paper, and about poor service by
post, telegraph, and railroad. Such difficulties in Yakutia or
Kamchatka need occasion no surprise, nor would they have done
much harm in view of the number of people involved, but what

can one say about breakdowns in areas within easy reach of Petersburg and Moscow or about the dragging out of the process in Petersburg and Moscow provinces themselves? Mogilev was no isolated province—it had swamplands, to be sure, but also the general headquarters of the Russian army—yet its returns disappeared without trace after being cast, counted, and sent in. Thus was lost to history one entire district. Kherson province in the Ukraine, among the most populous in the country and bordering the Black Sea, with the major urban center of Odessa, conducted its election so poorly that the *Russkiia Vedomosti* complained of the count as "dragging out interminably." It seems never to have been completed. Sviatitski assigns 694,391 votes to the district with the caution that this figure is incomplete and may not be accurate. Spirin gives 932,271, unacceptable because his totals for the main lists end in three zeroes, representing at best an estimate of unknown worth, and because his Menshevik and rightist votes clearly do not fit his expanded base, and so cast doubt on all the rest. My smaller total is 620,720, its advantage being that only real votes are included (no estimates or projections here), its disadvantage being that probably not more than half the vote is represented.

From this spectacle of incompetence it is a pleasure to turn to the neighboring province of Ekaterinoslav, where everything is as it should be—neat and cleaned up, complete and official. It, too, was a populous and important province with ethnic diversity and varied economic interests. But it had an electoral commission that could get things done. Its task was complex beyond measure: eight uezd commissions and five urban ones to supervise, 238 volosts and 1,052 precincts to organize, no fewer than fifteen competing lists to examine and certify, nearly 35 million units of printed matter to be prepared, those for the Jewish parties to be bilingual (a demand that caused the hard-pressed commission to lose its equanimity), and various public organizations to be mobilized for assistance in printing, cutting, sorting, packing, transporting, and distributing the election materials. Over-

hanging the whole procedure was the question whether there
would be enough money. The commission was fully conscious of
the fateful significance of this election in determining whether
Russia would achieve self-government, and proclaimed its intent
of having everything in readiness for the 25th of November. It
succeeded admirably in holding the election on time and without
a hitch, in counting and tabulating all 1,193,049 of the votes, in
drawing up the papers and sending them in before the Bolshevik
axe fell on the less competent All-Russian Commission.

In the contrast between the Ekaterinoslav and Kherson commissions can be seen the importance of the personal factor in
human affairs. How the former came into being under the Provisional Government is not easy to understand. By accident, one
may presume. The Kherson commission accords so much better
with the quality and attitude of the Provisional Government.
That authority may simply have been unable to make a better
choice. But what is obvious is that it did not care to make the
effort. The record is not clear as to whether the trouble arose
belatedly in Kherson province or whether, as is more likely, it
had been there all along. But there is no doubt concerning Egoriev uezd in the province of Riazan. It had failed to keep abreast
of its duties from the beginning. At the end, when Riazan had
done rather well and the eleven other uezds had reported, Egoriev uezd defaulted once more. Its commission should have been
discharged well beforehand and a new one appointed. The Provisional Government had devised a cumbersome system of rely-
ing on local, democratically recast organs to staff the electoral
process, yet when ill effects came to the fore, it still did not move
to better the situation.

The strung-out character of the election had disastrous conse-
quences. The Constituent Assembly receded from real to unreal
in the public consciousness and people began to ask themselves
whether it would even come into being, not to speak of escaping
death at Bolshevik hands. A separate peace, Ukrainian nationalism, and the rumblings of civil war engrossed public atten-

tion, not an election that would not end or a parliament that became more wraith-like by the day. The morale of both those who made use of the electoral machinery and those who staffed it was undermined. Voters saw less and less reason to go to the polls, election officials had less and less heart in what they were doing. Those in the north Caucasian district of Ter-Daghestan, where the voting had been first delayed and then spread out from 26 November to 5 December, counted the votes in some areas but did not bother to report them, and in other areas refrained even from counting them. And so we have figures for Vladikav- kaz and several other towns and garrisons but nothing at all from the back country, inhabited by valorous peoples speaking impos- sible languages, from which the results would have been among the most interesting in the whole country. Rough sledding had attended the campaign in the distant but important electoral district of Syr Darya, in which voting had been postponed till mid-December, then, after further delay, to the latter part of January 1918. The Tashkent Bolsheviks had planned an election rally for January 19 but on the previous day the boss in Pe- tersburg had put an end to the Constituent Assembly. No elec- tion was held. In the country as a whole things had gone so badly that it was only half an assembly that fell under Lenin's ban. The other half either had not been elected, had fallen by the wayside, or had not chosen to come (see my book *The Sickle under the Hammer*, chaps. VI–VIII and pp. 456–466). The Bolsheviks had only to administer the coup de grâce; the Provisional Govern- ment, by first depriving the assembly of a favorable conjuncture and then causing it to come into being in piecemeal fashion, had ensured its ruin.

There are those who contend that the situation both within the country and outside it precluded any satisfactory consultation of the population in 1917. This contention, made in exculpation of the Provisional Government, does not stand the test of history. Two months had been enough to enable France to choose its constituent assembly in 1848. Two months had sufficed for Germany (9 November 1918–19 January 1919). And two weeks had seen an election held and the Bordeaux assembly convened after the capitulation of Paris (29 January–13 February 1871). Eight months were required for Russia to *begin* to elect its constituent assembly and almost two more for *half* this assembly to convene. But, it will be objected, France and Germany are nation-states and limited in size, whereas Russia is an empire, vast and many-peopled. Actually Russia was in far better condition to elect an assembly in 1917 than France in 1871 or Germany in 1919, countries that were wholly at the mercy of enemy powers as well as being racked by revolution and Germany by near famine. For France even to hold an election required the indulgence of Bismarck. Russia had lost nothing except the outer belt of territories that it had taken from others; hardly anywhere did the enemy stand on truly Russian soil. It is not the unwieldiness or backwardness of Russia that accounts for the difference, it is the will of the respective governments. Those of France and Germany sincerely sought an expression of the national will because of democratic principle and as a means of coping with a desperate situation: that of Russia outwardly deferred to popular sovereignty but was determined to thwart or delay as long as possible anything that might detract from prosecution of the war. It quite failed to see that this course was creating for itself as well as for the assembly a situation that would become not only desperate but hopeless.

CHAPTER VIII

THE DEGREE OF VOTER PARTICIPATION

THE RESPONSIBILITY OF the Provisional Government for the fate that overtook the assembly is a matter not adequately treated in the earlier version of this book. Other matters stand in need of revision or correction.

One is the degree of participation in the election, alluded to above as being drawn down by the malfunctioning of the process, the intrusion of other concerns, and the fading prospects of the assembly. There is little hard information upon which to base a judgment. The Ministry of the Interior had estimated that the electorate numbered perhaps 90 million, yet almost at once the Provisional Government decided to plan on 100 million as affording a margin of safety. No one really knew how many citizens would be eligible to vote. But on the basis of this figure, and with 44 million, more or less, taken as the highest count of actual voters, the view has gained currency in Soviet literature that not even half the electorate was interested enough to cast a ballot. The view has not passed unchallenged, yet it dies hard. It is absurd, first, because in some districts no election was held, and second, because in many of those that reported, the vote is incomplete. On the other hand, the assertion in the *Russkiia Vedomosti* that in the rural areas a participation of 60 to 80 percent was the rule is too high. It was based on returns from the Central Black Earth provinces, where the election was held on time, in the first flush of enthusiasm aroused by the Socialist Revolutionaries, who were strong here and had gotten their message across to the peasants that they would get all the land from the Constituent Assembly and pay nothing for it. The newspaper gives 73 percent participation for Tambov province as a whole. The figure is high. It is also rare, for while the total vote is available for many provinces or districts, the number of citizens entitled to vote is given for very few, and then only in round numbers. And so only a few percentages can be cited here. At the head of the list, Tambov in the Central Black Earth zone is joined by Poltava in the Ukraine with 74 percent. At the lower end comes Tobolsk in western Siberia, with only 33.5 percent. The Soviet source is suspect, however, as the author is interested in belittling the overwhelming SR victory there by showing that its backing was actually quite slender. In between are three provinces on the middle Volga: Kazan, with a turnout of about 66 percent; Simbirsk, with 58 percent; and Samara, with 54.86 percent. Taurida province in the south—it included the Crimea—had an attendance at the polls of 54.74 percent. Unfortunately, information for other peasant provinces is not available.

It is reasonable to assume that the highest degree of political consciousness should have been found in the metropolitan electoral districts—there were only two in this peasant empire—and in truth, the showing there was satisfactory but certainly not sensational: in Petersburg 71 percent of the qualified citizens went to the urns and in Moscow 66.5 percent. Even here, where some exactitude could be expected, figures vary according to the source, from 69.7 percent to 72 percent in the case of Petersburg and from 65.4 percent to 69.7 percent in the case of Moscow— one more example, if any were needed, of the wretched organization of this election. Whatever the exact figures, they were much higher than those in numerous provincial towns; in Penza, unique because of precise information, of 49,741 with the right to vote, only 17,583 or 35 percent exercised it. Something is needed from the armed forces and in two instances may be provided. The Baltic Fleet cast 70 percent of its registered total (76 percent for the sailors, who were outnumbered by the soldiers and workers on the bases). The Northern Front cast 72.36482 percent, a figure exact to the last digit and also official. It is our prize electoral district and very important, for it was closest to the capital and had the Lettish riflemen.

And that is all. It is not enough. A sampling of 11 parts out of

80 cannot serve as a basis for judgment concerning the whole. Where knowledge leaves off, intuition takes over. On the basis of long familiarity with the subject and thorough study, I feel that the best estimate of the degree of participation in the election to the All-Russian Constituent Assembly is somewhere around 55 percent. It most likely does not exceed 60 percent and assuredly does not fall under 50 percent. And if the chosen figure errs, it does so on the conservative side. In this respect, therefore, the election resembles an American more than a European election. But under the circumstances that prevailed late in 1917 and early in 1918, and because the open ballot made it possible for nearly all shades of opinion to present their case to the public, it rises to a higher level.

CHAPTER IX

WERE THE ELECTION RESULTS
UNREPRESENTATIVE OF THE COUNTRY?

ANOTHER MATTER THAT needs to be set right concerns what might be termed the unrepresentative character of the election. Indictment on such grounds comes from two sides, from the right and from the left-center, a category that includes all those so-cialists or near-socialists who opposed the extremists (Bolsheviks or Left SRs), supported the Provisional Government, and wished to continue the war, for whatever reason. The rightists rejected the election, the assembly, and everything to do with both as being the result of Jewish, German, or criminal machinations that had beclouded the consciousness of the Russian people. To them these were temporary aberrations that would be dispelled. The Russians would then resume their devotion to throne and altar and all the other accursed peoples would be dragged back into union with Russia One and Indivisible. The left-center, as the ostensible winner at the polls, could not go in for such a blanket indictment and contented itself with disparaging the ex-tremist vote, much too large for comfort, by attributing it to soldier influence and hence destined to be ephemeral in view of the self-demobilization of the army. Whether the charge of unrepresentativeness comes from right or left-center, the effect is to tarnish the only real election in Russian history.

This tarnish must be cleaned off. In the earlier version I made a certain concession to this point of view; I now regret that I made any concession at all. Both what came before and what came after refute the charge of abnormality. Two elections held in 1906 and 1907 reveal that the country was thoroughly revolutionary, de-spite a restricted franchise. Only the travesty of the ensuing Stolypin franchise papered over the low estate of the old regime. In the light of the first revolution (1905–1907), the imperial gov-ernment's entrance into the world war was equivalent to signing its own death warrant. As for the period after the Constituent Assembly, there were no elections worthy of the name, either in Soviet Russia or in the territories controlled by the Whites. Everything was dictated from above, everything was cut and dried, the result preordained—with one exception. In late July of 1918 Vladivostok was permitted to elect a city council. Here a White regime had replaced Soviet rule as a consequence of Allied intervention, but it tolerated twenty lists on the ballot, one of which was that of the trade unions, dominated by the Bolsheviks and the Left SRs, whose collaboration lasted longer here than in European Russia because of the common danger from Japan, Great Britain, and the United States. The election was well attended, 77.4 percent of those eligible taking part. Of the 101 seats at stake, 53 went to this list, 22 to that of the Democratic Bloc of centrist and right-wing SRs together with the Mensheviks—the left-center mentioned above—and 26 to all the rest. For the Constituent Assembly the Bolsheviks had gotten 49 percent of the vote, the Left SRs 13.6 percent on separate lists, so that their combined share of the total vote had fallen off about 10 percent between November 1917 and July of the next year. In all likelihood the decline sprang not from the political setback—the Soviet regime had not come into power locally until after the November election—but simply from the melting away of the garrison attendant upon demobilization.

Even so, the extremist showing was impressive enough, more than half the whole, and that under a White government. The newspaper that is our source, of Constitutional Democratic tendency, had dealt with the election in muffled tones, presumably with an eye on the censorship, but now it came right out and voiced the obvious conclusion: Bolshevism has not been outlived, the workers are with it still. The dismayed authorities branded the outcome as illegal. The council was stillborn. Months later, at the end of December 1918, the full-blown reaction under Admiral Kolchak made another attempt to bring into being a docile city council in Vladivostok. This time the workers resorted to a boycott. It was inordinately successful. Of 37,384 electors, 4,115, or 11 percent; went to the polls. On this occasion many who were not workers decided not to participate in a farce. It was a very clear manifestation, not of the evanescence of extremist sentiment but of the shallowness of Kolchak's support. His strength lay in Great Britain.

To all those who would argue that one city does not a country make, the answer is that the whole course of the civil war bears testimony to the thoroughly revolutionary character of the country; not, of course, that all of this revolutionism can be specifically identified with Bolshevism by any means, for much of it was Socialist Revolutionary or nationalist or anarchist or simply nonpartisan. The Whites fought grimly and bravely, the conscripts under them not nearly so well, and it seems that they came as far as they did largely because of Allied backing, which had to compensate not only for the Whites' numerical inferiority but also for the stupidity of Russia One and Indivisible. The results of the election to the Constituent Assembly in no way contradicted Russian reality, in no way were out of character with the country. The election to the Constituent Assembly foreshadowed what the civil war would confirm.

Once that struggle was concluded, however, Bolshevism faced a new situation in which its excesses and exactions took their toll in a precipitous falling away of peasant support and the rise of the Green movement, which manifested itself in a wave of peasant uprisings, some of them of formidable proportions. Disaffection spread to the working class and racked the Baltic Fleet. Faced with a prospect that made him quail as the White armies never had, Lenin resorted to the New Economic Policy as a means of saving his regime.

A legitimate question is whether other parties could have held their lines as well as Bolshevism in the wake of the election to the Constituent Assembly. The Socialist Revolutionaries had amassed the largest vote and, according to a widespread misconception, had secured an absolute majority instead of a mere plurality. The SR following exceeded the Bolshevik by a ratio of 16 : 10 but was much softer. How cohesive it would have been had Russia continued down the road of democratic development on which it was started before the Bolsheviks knocked to pieces everything in opposition is something upon which the election can shed light—not so much the voting itself as the process behind it. Some features of the process have received brief attention, others have received none at all. I have dealt with the makeup of the official SR lists, particularly the overrepresentation of old-line Populists (Narodniki), in *The Sickle under the Hammer*, but at the time of the first version of this study I had neither the knowledge nor the maturity to grasp the significance of unofficial lists that were presented and largely turned down. Yet these unofficial lists hold the key to any judgment concerning the future of the country's largest party. For what is at stake is not the constancy or inconstancy of the "March SRs," all those recruits from the upper levels of society who, borne on the wave of revolution, found the SR label convenient, modish, and sufficiently ill defined to suit their purposes. What is at stake is the loyalty of the peasant following, of the element that was the party's reason for being.

Reports to the central or All-Russian electoral commission from subordinate commissions in the provinces reveal a surprising number of dissident peasant lists presented or "declared" for submission to the voting public in addition to, and in competition with, the official SR lists containing the names of the candidates of the "peasants' party." The presence of these rival lists was unexpected and has passed unnoted in literature on the subject. It also seems to have been unexpected by the authorities in 1917, and decidedly unwelcome. These authorities, through the zemstvos or otherwise, were themselves in very many instances SRs, accustomed to look upon SR tutelage of the peasant movement as a natural right. As a result, many of the off-color lists did not make it through the second stage of confirmation or "publication." They were disallowed for failure to meet the deadline or some other legal requirement, but one may be pardoned the suspicion that on occasion it was less the default of the petitioners than the disfavor of the officials that determined the issue. To be sure, these were peasant lists and may not have been drawn up with the care expended on qualifying papers for the major parties. In Kostroma province 15 lists were put forward but only 5 were accepted. Among those rejected were lists headed "Rural Society of So-and-So." The nature of these rural societies is not disclosed, but some if not all of them must have been peasant. As little or even less is known about other districts with numerous rejections. In Pskov, 4 of 13 lists were disallowed, in Volynia 17 of 30 (5 of the 17 are known, however—see below), in Voronezh half of the 16 presented were disqualified, in Penza 5 of 11 plus others presented too late, in Viatka 8 of 20, and in the Siberian districts of Tomsk and the Transbaikal, 3 out of 9 and 6 out of 15 respectively. The Samara electoral district far exceeded any other with its record of 95 lists turned in and 79 turned down, 42 because they had been received after the time had expired. About the only general comment concerning these lists in the provinces mentioned is that very many of them were of strictly local appeal, so it may be surmised that a good number were of peasant origin.

There is no need to speculate in certain cases where definite information is available concerning dissident peasant lists and their fate. One of these cases is the southwestern province (or district) of Volynia. Here no fewer than 5 lists identified as peasant were among the 17 that failed of acceptance; of the 12 others not identified, some are stated to have emanated from party dissenters, an origin that might make them peasant also if the party were Ukrainian SR or SR. Another such province or district was Novgorod, in the northwest, where four local peasant groups failed to qualify. Two such groups on the volost level in Smolensk, to the west of Moscow, had no better fortune. The provinces of Tver in the north, Taurida in the south, and Yenisei in Siberia each had a peasant group that sought to contest the election only to be denied a place. The one in Tver styled itself "farmer," a term that might be borrowed by landowners—in the sense of estate holders—to conceal their identify and attract a following not confined to aristocrats and landed capitalists. But inasmuch as the landowners had entered their own slate in this province under their own flag, we may conclude that the word "farmer" in this instance applied to better-to-do peasants who feared being submerged in the mass.

Most interesting of the electoral districts for which we have information about peasant lists is Vladimir, in the central industrial area northeast of Moscow. After it had announced that of the 11 lists of candidates submitted, 7 had passed muster but 4 remained in doubt, the commission later reported on the eve of the election that all of the doubtful lists, proposed by nonpartisan groups of peasant voters, had been disqualified. Without indicating the grounds for its action, it did make one highly significant statement—that even after the turndown, such lists continued to come in and were being ignored. Here the latent hostility of electoral commissions staffed by Populists and others, but especially by Populists, toward independent political activity on the part of peasants swims to the surface.

Despite the obstacles in their way and despite their own inexperience, some independent-minded peasant groups succeeded in getting their candidates before the voters. How did they fare? Not very well. For the present the thoughts of most peasants did not range beyond getting the land without compensation to private owners; how title would be vested was of little immediate concern, and consequently they were content to give their suffrage to the combined list of candidates of the SR party and the Soviet of Peasant Deputies (or the Ukrainian SR party and the Selians'ka Spilka) that was offered in nearly every electoral district. In the face of this attitude and this combination, an independent, nonpartisan peasant ticket operating on a provincial level could usually draw only some thousands of votes, and one operating at a strictly local level only some hundreds of votes.

Vitebsk province, in the west, is as good an example as can be
found: Peasants of Vitebsk Province received 9,752 votes, while
Peasants of Boletskii Volost of Gorodok Uezd drew 752, or together some 10,500 votes out of 560,538 cast, or not even 2
percent. It is true that ethnic diversity prevents a clear picture:
the Latgallian peasants in league with their Socialist Federalist
co-nationals drew 26,990 votes, but here nationality eclipses the
class factor. Yet Samara province on the Volga, decidedly Great
Russian despite sizable Tatar and German minorities, with almost twice the vote of Vitebsk yielded only 3,030 votes for its
nonpartisan peasant list and multinational Ufa province only
3,078, or almost exactly the same. No conclusions can be drawn
except that none of these efforts got anywhere or created more
than a ripple.

In respect to peasants' attempts to find their own way, mention should be made of the Peasant Union. It had been set up by
Socialist Revolutionaries at the time of the first revolution (1905–
1907) as a watered-down, nonpartisan front for the purpose of
appealing to a population supposedly repelled by the party's extremism, particularly its republicanism and practice of terrorism.
The Union experienced a certain revival in 1917 after the February or March revolution, despite its abandonment by the SRs in
favor of rural soviets as the approved form of organization for
the peasantry. The Union clung to its nonpartisanship and in
general to its renunciation of extremism, now expressed in support of the Provisional Government and the war, in condemna-
tion of the seizure of estates, and in suspected willingness to
consider a measure of compensation for at least some owners of
land to be taken away. The moderation that perhaps had been an
advantage in 1905 had certainly become a disability in 1917. The
position of the Union ensured that it would not be in the main-
stream of peasant development. Here and there the Union contested the polls with little result. Moscow province gave it 13,000
votes, one uezd missing, and Perm slightly more, mainly in
Krasnoufimsk uezd. Only in western Siberia did it make a show-

ing of consequence; here in Tobolsk province, in conjunction with the People's Socialists, it received 50,780 votes and elected one member of the assembly. It is not possible to say which component of the joint list contributed more to this modest success. Even in Tobolsk, however, the combination of the SR party (PSR) with the peasant soviets scored over seven times as many votes and elected nine deputies. The Peasant Union was out of the running; the tide of history had passed it by.

If independent action on the part of peasants were to get anywhere, their soviets had to break loose from the SR party and stand alone, free of partisan ties. Only the soviets had a broad enough base to make such action count. In three instances, two at either end of this vast empire that nevertheless was all in one piece, and the third at its very center, such a separation did take place: in Bessarabia, in the southwestern corner of European Russia; in the electoral district made up of the Amur region and the Maritime province, on the Pacific; and in the Uralsk district, in northwestern Turkestan. As ill luck would have it, all three pose grave problems for the scholar, yet it has been possible with great effort to assemble some information about them. Bessarabia remained one of the most intractable areas of investigation all the way down to 1964, when a Soviet study distinctly superior to most made an earnest effort to shed light on what happened there in 1917 in respect to the election and otherwise. With every advantage at hand except the passing of time, the Afteniuk collective managed to produce figures only for the town of Kishinev and for three of the eight uezds, not including the most populous ones. So limited a result despite the competence displayed indicates that the full story of 1917 in Bessarabia may never be told. Even so, we now have something where before there was nothing. The rupture between the SR party and the peasant soviets occurred in time to allow rival lists to be submitted to the electorate. They easily outdistanced the other 15 lists, the SRs running somewhat ahead of the peasant soviets with 33.6 percent of the vote as against 27.2 percent. It must be remembered that these figures are for only a part of Bessarabia, and the lesser part. It is strange that though there are no returns for the province as a whole, the delegates elected are known, and in this respect there was an even split between the SRs and the peasant soviets, each having 5 out of a total of 13.

Unfortunately, the result in Bessarabia cannot be viewed simply as confirmation of our thesis that peasants—in this case substantial numbers of them—were becoming restive under SR domination, for the cleavage between party and soviets was underlain by something else of equal or even greater importance—by national friction. The peasant soviets claimed to be nonpartisan but the predominant influence was that of Rumanian SRs, many of whom were fervent nationalists. It was the Ukraine all over again, only at a lower stage of development, because in Bessarabia the population was more inert and more illiterate. The ability of the SRs to vie on even terms with the peasant soviets in the November election is evidence of retention of a part of their "Moldavian" following, since the population of Bessarabia was 48 percent Rumanian and only 8 percent Russian (around 20 percent was Ukrainian). The cleavage is borne out by the very names of the delegates to the Constituent Assembly, those elected on the SR list being Russian or Jewish and those on the soviet list Rumanian. It is regrettable not to know what the Ukrainian peasantry did, if it were anything more than an inert mass—after all, its ethnic group was the second most numerous in the province—but the dereliction of the Provisional Government is nowhere better seen than in Bessarabia, which remains to this day a dark province in respect to the election.

Ethnic diversity is not a complicating factor in the Far East, where the Ukrainian was the only minority of any consequence, yet strife of a regional, ideological, and social character within the Socialist Revolutionary movement had by the fall of 1917 reached a level of intensity scarcely equaled elsewhere. The SRs on the Amur had parted company with those in the Maritime province although the two camps were of the same rosewater coloration, the left SRs in Vladivostok were at war with both, and the peasants' soviets of the Maritime region (not of the Amur) had run up the banner of independence from partisan influence and gone their own way. It is the latter development that is of concern here. The second Maritime Regional Congress of Soviets of Peasant Deputies—titles were heavy in 1917—had convened from 30 September to 3 October 1917, nearly two months in advance of the election, with 564 delegates in atten- dance. So it was a real peasants' congress, not stacked with or by intellectuals. The first day witnessed a rout of the SRs: certain of their members who were proposed for the presidium were thrown down, and peasant speaker after peasant speaker argued that only peasants should be sent to the Constituent Assembly, not SRs. In other words, this was a revolt against domination by intellectuals. The second day saw the SRs cajole the majority of the peasants back into submission. Thereafter a gap in the sources prevents our following developments, but the upshot is clear: hostility reasserted itself and this time led to a clean break. The four-way split in SR ranks duly resulted in four competing lists at the polls. The election was held on schedule in spite of the 9,612 kilometers between Vladivostok and Petersburg, yet an- other demonstration, as in the case of Ekaterinoslav, that local effort could offset the slackness of the Provisional Government. Only in the trackless wastes north of the Amur did trouble arise; there at the time of the tabulation used in this study—much superior to any other—312 voting places had reported and 77 had not, of which nearly 50 are said to have held no election at all. Thus in spite of prolonged effort and numerous sources, this fascinating district remains incomplete, and if the last assertion is true it will ever remain so.

List no. 2, that of the peasant soviets of the Maritime province standing alone, came in first with 56,718 votes, or 27 percent of the total for the entire district. The Maritime SRs, bereft of their rural following, got only 6,513, whereas the Amur SRs, suc- cessful in retaining theirs, placed second with 41,152 votes, or

nearly 20 percent of the total. The Bolsheviks pressed them hard
with 19.5 percent, well ahead of the Cossacks in fourth position
(10.8 percent) and well over twice as strong as Constitutional
Democrats or Mensheviks, both of whom nevertheless did better
here than usually. The left-wing SRs could muster only 5,805
votes as a distinctly urban group, in contrast to the situation in
European Russia, where they were a peasant party not wanting
in support among workers and soldiers, notably in Petersburg. It
may be noted that in the Far East, as everywhere else, peasants
and Cossacks never coalesced despite their common agricultural
interest, for the peasants were levelers; they resented the generous landed endowment of the Cossacks and felt that their land
should go into the common pot for redistribution.

The result of the November election on the Amur and in the
Maritime province shows that peasants organized in soviets and
striking out on their own could achieve a measure of success even
in 1917 when the matter at issue was getting possession of the
land rather than the way it was to be held later, in the postrevo-
lutionary era. Already in 1917 the dissident groups, small numerically but widely distributed over the country, which were seeking to participate in the election to the Constituent Assembly
betray a desire on the part of the peasants to manage their own
affairs independently of Populist (Narodnik) leadership (the SRs
were the main Populist movement). On the surface this desire
bespeaks, first, the distrust or outright dislike that simple people
feel for those who talk down to them from an intellectual emi-
nence, and second, an inclination to form a special-interest group
that would seek to exploit others as the peasants themselves had
been exploited. Underneath, however, something far more significant was involved. A small minority of peasants was already
looking beyond expropriation of estates without compensation
toward the way the land would be held once it was in their
possession. Some already held more land than the average and
wished to protect it against leveling by the mass. All sought
security for what they had or would get. These peasants,

whether they realized it or not, were groping their way toward an order of private ownership. Consciously or subconsciously they were preparing to burst the bonds of a collectivist ideology that intellectuals had thought to foist upon them but that never had become firmly rooted.

In one electoral district this process of emancipation was already out in the open. List no. 2 in Poltava province represented those who advocated with all the vigor at their command the private ownership of peasant holdings. It is branded the landowners' list by Ukrainian Socialist Revolutionary (USR), SR, and Soviet sources alike; it was so branded by Sviatitski; following their example, I so denominated it in the 1950 version of this study. It is a false classification. The real designation of the list is Farmers-Owners (*Khleboroby sobstvenniki*). To be sure, estate owners might adopt some such name for their list as a protective coloration and also as a means of widening their appeal—that is, of attracting plebeian support. But in this instance the objective facts argue otherwise. The highest vote that a real landowners' list drew was registered in the neighboring province of Ekaterinoslav, where 26,597, or 2.2 percent, favored list no. 1, Landowners and Nonpartisan Progressives, headed by M. V. Rodzianko, leader of the Octobrists and presiding officer of the imperial Third and Fourth Dumas, elected on the Stolypin franchise, whose presence at the head of anything would have made it rightist. Otherwise, the landowners did not fare so well. Only some half a dozen districts gave them between 11,000 and 14,000 votes, and in the rest the center of gravity seemed to be between 7,000 and 8,000. In most districts they had no lists. In those where they did, their share of the total vote was around 1 percent. Poltava province, on the other hand, gave the farmers 5.3 percent or 61,115, only 3,345 behind the third-place Bolsheviks. Had this been truly a landowners' list, its showing would have been out of line with the performance of landowners in every other district in the country.

A further consideration is the tenor of the campaign. It had taken the form of a fight, and a very bitter fight, between the dominant Ukrainian SRs—or rather the Selians'ka Spilka, the peasant organization linked to them as the peasant soviets were to the Russian SRs—and the numerically much inferior farmers' list. The Left SRs were tolerated; the Bolsheviks and Constitutional Democrats were here too weak to arouse much animosity, the former having strength only in garrisons, which were demoralized, and the latter having no strength. So the lightning hit the partisans of the farmers' list, against whom all manner of discrimination and intimidation were practiced, including threats of violence from roving bands of soldiers. That such threats were not empty is seen in a bloody action that took place in Konstantinograd uezd. A leading organizer of the farmers, one Kovalenko (initials unknown), had survived the election, but not for long. A band of soldiers invaded his home in January 1918, "arrested" (i.e., seized) him, led him out to a field, and shot him. He had stood out against the herd and paid for it with his life. Almost nothing is known of him, but it seems safe to say that he was Ukrainian and that he came from the people—that is, that he was dangerous to the would-be shepherds.

Why did the Spilka and its allies, the USRs, waste so much wrath on the farmers-owners' movement? For three reasons: first, it broke the ranks of Ukrainian unity; second, it menaced their monopoly control of the rural population; third, it posed a mortal threat to their collectivist ideology. Had it been a front for landowners, as they and others insisted it was, they need not have been concerned about it, for nothing was surer than that landowners were not going anywhere in 1917. But it was a genuine peasants' movement—better-to-do peasants, it is true—and it had prospects for the future, when peasants in general might turn in the direction it wanted to go. The intensity of the hostility that greeted it is the best argument for the plebeian character of the farmers-owners' movement. The Spilka-USR people should have paid more attention to Bolshevism, but such was its rootlessness in Poltava that they became nearsighted in relation to it and could not see farther afield. For them the danger came from the farmers-owners, from list no. 2. And in a sense they were right. Kovalenko came on the scene too early. It is always dangerous to anticipate history, for you may not be around when your anticipation is confirmed. A few years later, under the New Economic Policy, which peasant uprisings in the form of the Green movement had wrested from the hands of the peasant-hating Lenin, numbers of these Spilka members and Ukrainian SRs were on the way to becoming what Kovalenko had wanted them to be—kulaks.

Returning now to the point of departure, to the indictment of the November election as registering a volatile or unnatural mood destined soon to pass and leave Russia free to return to her traditional moorings, we have seen that the backing of Bolshevism was anything but ephemeral. But what about the Socialist Revolutionaries, ostensibly the winners of the election—would not their following have gone elsewhere, once the peasants had divided up the estates and in general had leveled landholdings? The election that gave them a plurality also revealed cracks that could widen into cleavage in the future. Would not a clean break have ensued between a party committed to collectivism and a peasantry in possession of all land and increasingly desirous of holding it as private property? Not necessarily. The official SR position was that the peasants should hold land as they pleased, either through the village community or individually, until such time as they realized the advantage of collective working of the land (the SRs in their naive faith were quite incapable of realizing how much time that would take). Forced collectivization, as under Joseph Stalin, had been ruled out from the start. But the peasants would only hold the land, they would not own it, for the land was to be a "belonging of all the people" (*obshchenarodnoe dostoianie*), whatever that might mean.

The time would come, however, when it would no longer be possible to cloud the issue in such nebulous phrases, or in terms so "*vide et sonore,*" as Metternich had said—in private—of the

Holy Alliance. The SRs would have to choose between their following and their ideology. The Bolsheviks, of course, made it unnecessary for them to choose by putting an end to them as an organized movement. Yet there is little doubt as to what they would have done had Russia continued on a democratic path. They would have followed their following and shed their ideology. Lenin had always insisted they were not socialists but only revolutionary democrats, when he did not call them something worse, and most likely he was right. Even the Left SRs would probably have done the same. They were closely bound to their peasant adherents and would have moved with them. It was not the Treaty of Brest Litovsk that lay at the root of their trouble with the Bolsheviks, as is so often asserted, it was the Leninist doctrine of the second social war in the village that caused the rupture in March of 1918 and bloodshed in July.

To conclude, there was nothing fundamentally wrong with this election. It reflected no momentary aberration on the part of the population but rather the broadness, depth, and power of the revolution set off against the weakness of its foes. It showed the situation as it was with indications of what would come later. It showed that the Bolsheviks were strong but not strong enough to govern democratically, even had they so desired; that the Socialist Revolutionaries eventually would have to give up their make-believe collectivism or go down; that the nationalism of the peoples lashed by Russification had been strengthened, not weakened; that the war was washed out. What more could reasonably be expected of an election? It has suffered from a campaign of disparagement launched by enemies on the left and on the right, understandably disgruntled over its results: by the Bolsheviks, who were denied democratic sanction for their rule, and by the reactionaries, who had their weakness exposed in all its nakedness.

CHAPTER X

QUESTIONS OF COMPILATION

IT REMAINS NOW to deal with the tabulations presented in Part Three: to contrast the results of my efforts with those of Sviatitski in 1918 and Spirin in 1968 (the only other tabulations of consequence), to note the successes achieved and the failures encountered, and to consider whether, and under what circumstances, further progress might be made. The outpourings of Soviet literature on the fortieth and fiftieth anniversaries of the revolution of 1917, in between and later on, particularly the studies of individual provinces for that year, awakened hope that election returns long missing or incomplete might be found and a truly satisfactory set of figures be submitted to public view. The hope was not realized. The provincial studies were written to prescription, mention of the election being neither proscribed nor encouraged; many authors preferred to pass it over in order to concentrate on happenings in the soviets, a safer topic. Some gave perfunctory attention to the election and sought to protect themselves by a one-sided presentation or by outright trickery: for example, they would play up the Bolshevik victory in Kharkov city, then later refer simply to the victory in Kharkov, leaving the reader with the impression that the victory referred to the entire province, whereas the truth of the matter is that in the province as a whole the joint list of the Left and Ukrainian SRs had swamped the Bolsheviks in the ratio of 7 to 1. Other accounts provide information but nothing that was not already known. And a very few advance our knowledge of the subject, as inconspicuously as possible, in an offhand manner within the text or buried in a footnote or an appendix.

Inspection of the materials was a frustrating experience, for it was soon evident that a cursory examination would be fruitless and even a thorough one productive only in rare instances. It must have resembled prospecting in the Old West: much digging and washing and little return, only a modest nugget here and there, never a lode. Just enough to keep going.

Finding less than expected in the new materials, I turned back to the metropolitan press of late 1917 into 1918, armed with a much better sense of what would be truly significant. Again the result was disappointment. For the most part it was a question not of having overlooked something the first time but simply of not enough being there. In general, newspaper coverage of the event ranged from poor to abominable. Distraction by other developments was a factor; a more important one was lack of basic pride in completeness and accuracy. The amazing failure to print satisfactory returns for Petersburg and Moscow provinces is to be explained, I think, by the painfulness of recording signal Bolshevik successes in both; the upper classes had been living in a fool's paradise, somehow believing that despite everything the peasantry was innately conservative, and the shock of disillusionment provided by the election was more than they could bear. Why *Pravda* also should have neglected these returns is something that has no explanation unless it be that the torturous count was more than it could bear. In partial exculpation of the non-Soviet press, however, it must be borne in mind that it was being hounded during the counting stage of the election by the Bolsheviks, now in power. The single most disastrous action in respect to the compilation of returns came on 27 November 1917, with the suppression of the *Russkoe Slovo*, published in Moscow by I. D. Sytin. This journal stood head and shoulders above others in assembling data and, whatever one may think of its "bourgeois" character, in striving for accuracy. Its death left a void that was not to be filled.

As to the provincial press, something will be said about it at the end.

A person engaged in research should be able to build upon the work of others in the same or related fields as he develops his own contribution. The tabulation accompanying the first version of this study was based upon the pioneer work of N. V. Sviatitski, published in 1918, to which additions and changes were made. The new tabulation owes little to him beyond what was already incorporated in the earlier one. It also owes little to the compilation made fifty years later by the Soviet historian L. M. Spirin, despite its ambitious character and the advantage of access to the central archives, an advantage presumably denied to Sviatitski and certainly to me. Spirin appreciably extended Sviatitski's achievement, producing returns for 65 districts instead of 54 and raising the total vote from 36,257,960 to 44,433,309, the latter by presenting fuller returns for certain districts included in Sviatitski's tabulation as well as by adducing eleven new districts. And yet it is possible to adopt only a small part of his additional material because he has permitted himself liberties no true scholar can take, with the result that too much of what he has done is untrustworthy when it is not downright wrong.

Some examples are in order. Spirin is hopelessly at sea in dealing with the SR vote in Kharkov province. The vote was huge and the province one of the most important in what had been the Russian empire. So his error here is no small matter. The SRs were divided into three camps. The left wing predominated and had the party organization firmly in hand. The right or pro-war SRs bolted and offered their own list of candidates, headed by E. K. Breshko-Breshkovskaia. This old-line Populist of the 1870s, known as "the grandmother of the Russian revolution," was now very much displeased by the way her grandchild had turned out. As for the Ukrainian SRs, they had formed a separate party some time earlier; they were now in communion, however, with the Left SRs, with whom they had agreed on a joint list for the assembly. Into this situation enters L. M. Spirin. He turns over the SR column to the 42,331 votes he adduces for the splinter list on the right. The 795,558 for the joint list he puts in the dumping column headed "Petit Bourgeois Nationality" (lists), whatever that means; here it means Ukrainian SR. By now, having thus disposed of some 80 percent of the total vote, he has thoroughly garbled the results in Kharkov province. The SR column belongs to the Left SRs as the official party organization in this province, but as their vote is inseparable from that of the Ukrainian SRs, it cannot properly be assigned to either party; the only solution is to put the letters JL (for "joint list") in both columns and the vote in the indivisible residue. It is a vexing situation, but to turn the SR column over to a splinter list is wholly inadmissible.

A similar situation existed in Kherson province, except that here there was no deviant list from the right. Again the Left SRs were in the saddle and again they were in union with the Ukrainian SRs. This time Spirin switches the vote for the joint list to the SR column so that it can be said that he is even-handed in his ineptitude. Inconsistency of the same order can be seen in relation to two other provinces. Mogilev, as I pointed out earlier, was the province of lost returns. Sviatitski had resorted to a purely artificial formula for determining its vote, which Spirin quite rightly refuses to accept. Sviatitski has used precisely the same formula to fill the void in the case of the Caucasian Front; his purely hypothetical figures Spirin adopts without so much as a murmur. Thus 420,000 votes are to be stricken from his tabulation without more ado. Still another inconsistency is seen in the treatment of the Social Democratic vote in Vologda and Tobolsk, provinces where the split between Bolsheviks and Mensheviks dating from 1903 had not yet taken place when the lists were drawn up; consequently there was in each case only a common list for both factions that were now becoming separate parties. Spirin places Vologda's SD votes in the Bolshevik column, whereas the SD votes in Tobolsk are treated as Menshevik. We know from the sequel that Bolsheviks predominated in Vologda but some SDs were Mensheviks, and to classify them all as Bolsheviks is to do violence to the truth. In general Spirin's treatment of joint lists is unsatisfactory.

There are other imperfections. Spirin seems not to be aware of the role of the peasant soviets in the Maritime province—that is, of the political movement that placed first in the election. The results he gives are defective. His figures for Perm province contain half a dozen errors, several of them minor but others substantial. At times he substitutes estimates for actual figures, as in the case of the Left and Ukrainian SRs, the Bolsheviks, and the Constitutional Democrats in Kherson province, all of whose vote totals end in three zeros; after so inflating the returns, he goes back to whatever he can scrape together for parties apparently not included in the estimate, with the curious result that from a base over 300,000 larger than mine he actually has fewer votes for three lists (Menshevik, Orthodox, and rightist). A resort to estimates also occurs in respect to Kazan and the Taurida, although the inflationary effect is less marked in these instances. To turn to estimates is to tread on slippery ground; in the present study only votes actually cast are counted, even if that means recording many fewer.

The advantage of access to the archives seems to have inspired in L. M. Spirin a certain disdain for published sources, for he is less thorough in their use than is advisable, even from the standpoint of his own interest. Drawing on the central archives, he has produced returns from the Kaluga and Semirechie districts, hitherto lacking, but these returns are not complete, as will be seen from a comparison with those in my tabulation, derived from provincial studies. There is nothing sacrosanct about archives, they also can err. They do not help him in respect to the military districts (except for the Baltic Fleet), where he is wholly dependent on Sviatitski, although unnecessarily so for the Northern Front, since a perfect set of returns for that district was printed in the most obvious and most authoritative source of all. As it is, he presents only three out of eight figures, all three ending in four zeros. These are no figures. As to the other fronts, for which any investigator depends on Sviatitski, no progress whatever having been made since his day, Spirin worsens matters by using Sviatitski's article in a compendium instead of his more detailed book, published in Moscow in 1918; as a result, this Soviet histo-

rian cannot give even the Menshevik vote in the army, significant on the more remote fronts.

As a result of these deficiencies and of others unmentioned,
with 15 districts unsatisfactory and others questionable out of a
total of 65, it seemed prudent not to borrow any findings from L.
M. Spirin unless they were at least partially confirmed by other
sources. As a consequence, the tabulation in Part Three owes
little to him beyond the Uralsk district, where we know at least
that his classification is correct, and the Constitutional Democratic vote in Orel province. On the other hand, his figures for
the Tula and Riazan districts have not been taken, even though
it seems reasonable to assume that they include the missing uezd
and volost in Tula and the missing uezd in Riazan, because no
confirmation could be found elsewhere. Nor can they be taken
for Viatka, a remote but populous province in the northeast,
despite the appearance of being plausible and complete, since
supporting evidence could not be discovered for a district that
exhibited all the faults of the electoral process before, during,
and after the voting. My tabulation has complete returns only for
the two Marxist parties and for the "Black Hundreds," as Soviet
sources term the Orthodox list, but my figures are not Spirin's
and the discrepancy must be resolved in favor of the local sources
I have used. Thus Spirin's access to the archives does not advance knowledge of the subject as much as might have been
hoped.

In general his work and Sviatitski's suffer from two overriding
faults: insufficient attention to classification of competing lists
and a pronounced tendency to ease the burden by instituting a
dumping column to accommodate—that is, to suppress—minor
lists even when these minor lists are locally of very considerable
importance. Sviatitski is less at fault in respect to classification
with his unrivaled knowledge of the subject—he was in the thick
of the campaign and was himself elected deputy from Kharkov
province—but he makes errors and Spirin makes more in a matter about which it can be said that it is scarcely less important to

know what voting is for than to know its numerical result. It is obvious that neither has studied the subject with the aid of the excellent and very informative bulletins issued before the election by the All-Russian Electoral Commission. Spirin dodges many classification difficulties with the aid of his dumping column headed "Others" and then goes further to create two more semi-dumping columns for the non-Russian nationalities with the headings "Petit Bourgeois Nationality" (lists) and "Bourgeois Nationality" (lists), thereby securing the double advantage of splitting up the total nationality vote and obscuring the vote of the individual nationalities. In this work of political obfuscation, however, he sometimes blurs his own perception, as when in Chernigov province he puts a Ukrainian "bourgeois" list with 12,650 supporters in his general dumping column (perhaps he did not know it was Ukrainian). If ignorance dictates some mistaken classifications, prejudice dictates others, as in the previously noted case of the peasant proprietors' list in Poltava province and also in the case of the major Moslem party in the Transcaucasus, the Müsavat (Equality), characterized by Spirin in 1968 as a "bourgeois nationality" party and in 1977 as "bourgeois reactionary." Bourgeois it may have been, Tatar nationalist it certainly was, but reactionary it was not. Its very name denoted its stand in favor of freedom for women, a position that had drawn down upon its head the hatred of the rival Ittihad or Moslem Union of Russia and the anathema of a turbaned cleric in the Taze Pir mosque of Baku, who denounced it as a godless and immoral movement.

It must be conceded that classification can be difficult. Right-wing Moslem groups may with equal justice be considered to belong to the religious category or be placed in the nationality column. Both elements in their dual nature stand out, sometimes the religious outweighing the secular. In this study they are nevertheless ranked by nationality: the Tatars on the Volga and in the Ural region denounced the Bashkirs for breaking Islamic unity by entering lists in competition with their own, but the indignation is very definitely colored by Tatar disdain of Bashkir claims to be a separate nationality, so that it is hard to say whether Tatar chauvinism or concern for a united religious front has here the upper hand. But in the case of the Bashkirs themselves there is no doubt as to the supremacy of nationalism. Nor is there in the case of the Tatar left, more numerous than the right, where more was involved than nationalism in the welling up of revolutionary sentiment for a better land deal, for social equality, and, above all, for an end to a hateful war. In the Moslem areas, therefore, only the right causes hesitation in respect to categorization.

Other difficulties arise in treating a subject so broad and complex. In the province of Poltava a list was entered that had no name. How is a list without name to be classified? Especially when the single bit of information concerning it occurs in a Soviet source that says it was "wild"—a colorful but not helpful description. For Sviatitski or Spirin there is no problem; their dumping column is waiting and functions in this as in many other instances of greater importance. My tabulation perforce has a residue column, but it has been my constant endeavor to keep it as small as possible. And Poltava is a perfect district: complete, official, with everything cleaned up and in place—a standing reproach to the Provisional Government as to what might have been. Rather than have this model province disfigured by an entry in the residue column, I decided to put it with the special-interest groups—after all, a phantom list should have a special interest.

The second overriding fault of the other two compilations—unwillingness to deal with minor parties—may spring from either sloth or prejudice. The latter is evidenced by the treatment of religious groups, the very mention of which irked the SR statistician Sviatitski in 1918 and the Soviet historian Spirin in 1968, and by the slighting of the less prominent nationality or special-interest groups, not to speak of the independent peasant movement already noted. While the showing of religious elements in the election was everywhere mediocre or weak, they here and there made a stand and the results deserve to be reported. Few are. The relative success of the Christian Union for Faith and Fatherland in Nizhni Novgorod elicits comment; the better-than-usual poll for both Orthodox and Old Believers in Perm does not. As an exception, the substantial backing of the Orenburg Cossacks is brought out, but the same favor is not extended to the Bashkirs of the same province, whose backing was also substantial, somewhere in the neighborhood of 100,000. By all odds the worst example of withholding information about nationality lists is seen in the Transcaucasus, the largest electoral district in the country, where to this day the votes for the Tatar Müsavat and the Armenian Dashnaktsutiun have not been disclosed. The ostensible excuse seems to be that since these parties did not have All-Russian followings but were of regional significance only, they do not merit the same consideration as parties of broad appeal. Yet within this region they were far more significant than the SRs, the Bolsheviks, or the Constitutional Democrats, disposing as they did of followings five times as numerous as these "All-Russian parties." The real reason for keeping the record under wraps, I suspect, is that to reveal the strength of national sentiment manifested in a real election for these two movements on the fringe of the Soviet empire is considered to be not in the interest of the Soviet regime.

The suppression, or rather the burial, of less eminent political groups through the medium of a dumping device lessens the benefit to be derived from a study of the subject even if it is occasionally relieved by special mention of this or that discard. Taken together with faulty classification, in all too many instances it impairs the value of the compilations made by Sviatitski and Spirin. In preparing Table 1 of this volume I have devoted much time to a study of the lists presented and those not presented in order to deepen our understanding of the election as well as to establish the correct relationship among the many contestants and to get each in the right position. Regrettably, it has not been possible to single out lists of limited significance for display in the master tabulation (Table 1) without overtaxing the reader's attention; it was decided that twelve columns of figures would be the limit, so that it has been necessary on occasion to combine several lists in a single column under a general heading. Under the heading "Special-interest groups," for example, will be found peasant lists entered as such, Cossacks, landowners, business groups, employees' associations, nonpartisans, and sundry elements with axes to grind, such as feminists. Within the column headed "Other socialist parties" are lumped together People's Socialists (NS) fused with the Group of Toil, Plekhanov's Unity, cooperatives, SR splinter groups of left and right, pro-war socialist blocs, and in general anything that is socialist and small except Menshevik factions, which by special dispensation are kept together in their own column so that they will amount to at least something. Several other columns also accommodate multiple listings (ethnic columns, religious and/or rightist, and of course the residue). Tables 2–5 expand several of these columns so that the vote for the individual lists contained in them can be seen; thus information withheld from other compilations can be found here.

CHAPTER XI

FAILURES AND SUCCESSES

AND NOW TO go into the tabulation itself, to see what has been done and what could not be done, to point out the more disheartening failures and the more signal successes, and to weigh the prospects of advancing knowledge of the subject beyond the present stage. In the 80 electoral districts that made up most of what had been the Russian Empire, somewhere in the vicinity of 50 million votes may have been cast. L. M. Spirin produces returns from 65 of these districts with a total of 44,433,309 votes. My tabulation consists of 70 districts (all 80 are listed) and 44,218,555 votes. Despite appearances, it is larger than his because from Spirin's total 420,000 for the Caucasian Front must be stricken without more ado as reflecting a purely arbitrary estimate made by Sviatitski (I have only the returns for the garrison of Erzerum fortress, 16,824, but these are real figures). Other deductions, as from Kherson province, where the main parties are assigned numbers terminating in three zeros, would be in order if there were any way of measuring them. Even so, the respective totals are remarkably close for figures that have been arrived at over such different roads, so close as to suggest that about all that is feasible has been wrung out of the sources available under present circumstances.

By all odds the most resounding failure in assembling our tabulation has been the Transcaucasian electoral district, the largest and very nearly the most difficult of all. It consists of half a dozen provinces and three major ethnic regions, and why the Provisional Government lumped them all as one electoral district defies comprehension unless it was to dull the effect of a spectacular showing on the part of the dominant nationalities if the area were divided into ethnic regions. The election exhibited all the unevenness that we have encountered elsewhere, the western section (Georgia) moving ahead and the eastern (Azerbaidzhan) lagging behind. Soon the process bogged down in a welter of conflicting reports that reflected various stages of voting and, more particularly, of counting. Such confusion arose that to this day people are not sure which set of returns corresponds more faithfully to the truth. Three have figured more prominently than others: one emanating from the Archives of the October Revolution (AOR), published in 1930, on the basis of a total vote of 1,887,453; the second advanced by Vladimir Voitinsky in his *Démocratie géorgienne* (Paris, 1921), based on a total of 1,996,263; and, more recently, a third stemming ultimately from an Armenian newspaper, the *Arev* of Baku, issue of 23 March 1918, based on 2,445,270 votes in all.

None of them is satisfactory. The most attractive is the third: it has all fifteen of the lists and in proper order, the figures are precise, the classifications correct, and the base of nearly 2.5 million participants is much broader than any other. That is the trouble, in fact; it is too broad. It has been promoted in the United States by R. J. Hovannisian and R. G. Suny and has caught on elsewhere, being adopted even by L. M. Spirin in a later work (1977) after he had used the AOR figures in his 1968 tabulation. But I have decided it cannot be used for reasons now to be set forth.

Amid any number of sources filled with claptrap and barren of worthwhile information there is one worthy of respect, by an author with a name honored in the annals of Georgian Bolshevism: N. B. Makharadze, *Pobeda sotsialisticheskoi revoliutsii v Gruzii* (Tbilisi, 1965). Pointing out that preparations for the election began too late in a district much too large, that the rolls of eligible voters were made up in haste, and that the campaign was not adequately provided for in either the technical or the material sense, Makharadze observes that the "information on the election in the Transcaucasus provided in the periodical press and other literature of that time varies substantially from one source to another," and concludes that "our historical literature has not shed light on the question of the election to the Constituent Assembly." He could say that again! Makharadze wades through the welter of misinformation, knocks down one bloated claim after another—all the more convincingly because some are slanted in favor of his own party—and ends by refusing to submit any statistics of his own in the face of the sheer hopelessness of deciding what is less far from the truth. He indicates a slight preference for the AOR findings. With this he sets the cross over the question, not, however, without giving one figure as a kind of lodestone to the floundering scholar. He states, on the authority of material in the Central State Historical Archives of the Georgian SSR, that the number of electors (i.e., qualified voters) in the Transcaucasus reached 3.5 million, thus giving us a means of operation.

Applying it to the three sets of returns mentioned above, we find that for the first (AOR, 1930) the degree of participation in the election was 54 percent, for the second (Voitinsky, 1921) 57 percent, and for the third (Armenian newspaper, 1918) 70 percent. Either the first or the second fits easily into the framework of the estimate made earlier of around 55 percent as the average for the country. But to accept the third would be to elevate the Transcaucasus to the level of Petersburg and Moscow in respect to political consciousness and interest in the election. To regard the Georgian and Armenian segments of the population as having attained such a level is not easy; so to regard the Moslem segment is impossible. Yet it is precisely this segment that causes the trouble, for the total Moslem vote of 926,905 is too large. The Georgian Menshevik vote is also too large. Right here may be one source of trouble. I strongly suspect, though I cannot prove, that Himmet ("Zeal," "Endeavor"), the Moslem SD organization (list 11), has been counted twice, once for the Mensheviks (list 1) and once by itself. If so, elimination of the duplication would reduce the vote for all lists by 84,743. Voitinsky has also erred in assigning Himmet to the Mensheviks, but at least he does not count it twice. Actually, his mistake is in a sense pardonable, as

our Tatar source (Mehmet-Zade Mirza-Bala, *Millî Azerbaycan
hareketi i Millî Azerbaycan "Müsavat" Halk Fırkası tarihi
[Fırka divani tarafindan neşrolunmuştur]* [n.p., 1938], p. 106)
says that Himmet consorted with the Mensheviks and turned its
back on the other Azerbaidzhan parties. Nevertheless, Himmet
had its own list and must be counted separately.

This party of zeal is not the only source of trouble, or even the
main source; whatever is done with it, the Moslem total is still
much too large. Something is wrong with the many votes assigned to the Moslem Socialist Bloc (list 12), for it is not apparent
where they could have come from. The only detailed returns at
our disposal are from parts of Baku province, in which this party
had only a negligible following; it obtained 903 votes in the city
and industrial suburbs, 96 in the rest of Baku uezd, 5 in all of
Lenkoran uezd, and 18 in Gökchai. This grand total of 1,022
votes is a far cry from the 159,770 credited to the party by the
Armenian newspaper. If these Moslem socialists were so few in
the Baku area, the main industrial area of the Transcaucasus
and the only industrial area of its Moslem part, where were the
rest of them to be found? The Ittihad ("Union") or Moslems of
Russia on the right also causes trouble but of the opposite kind. It
is credited in the Armenian newspaper with a strength of 66,505,
yet in our very limited area of detailed returns it already has
49,796 and, with the rest of Baku province and all of Elisavetpol
and Erevan provinces out, it should certainly exceed the allotted
sum, probably by a wide margin. More serious, however, is the
question of by far the largest Moslem party, Müsavat, really the
voice of Tatar nationalism. It is given 615,816 votes, over
200,000 more than Voitinsky's figure of 405,917; the archival
source (AOR) and other Soviet sources withhold the vote for
Müsavat and its Armenian counterpart, as previously noted.
Where the truth lies it is impossible to say, though the report in
the Armenian newspaper appears to be too high. Whatever the
absolute figure, the proportion of the total Moslem vote represented by ballots for Müsavat seems to be low, for both the

Armenian paper and Voitinsky have it to be about two-thirds, whereas our Tatar source, published by the Müsavat party council in exile, asserts it was 75 to 80 percent (p. 102).

And so we give up on the Moslem vote in the Transcaucasus, the main though not the only obstruction to compiling satisfactory returns. Noah Zhordaniia, the boss of Georgian Menshevism, explained the delay in setting up an authority counter to the Soviet in terms of the dragging out of the election in the eastern Transcaucasus (the Moslem areas); not before mid-December, he had said on November 24, would action be feasible. As a matter of fact, it was only on 23 January 1918 that he could move decisively toward erecting a new organ of power on the basis of the representation elected to the Constituent Assembly (G. I. Uratadze, *Obrazovanie . . .Gruzinskoi Demokraticheskoi Respubliki* [Munich, 1956], pp. 27, 45).

This representation offers another way of getting at the truth besides the effort to determine the degree of participation as a means of testing conflicting claims. The AOR or Soviet publication of 1930 sought to compensate for giving up on tabulating the vote by putting together as complete a list as possible of the deputies elected to the Constituent Assembly. Here it enjoyed a high degree of success. For the Transcaucasus it lists 14 members for the Mensheviks (already in effect the party of Georgian nationalism and soon to become so openly), 12 members for four Moslem parties, 10 for the Armenian Dashnaktsutiun, 2 for the SRs, and 1 for the Bolsheviks. This distribution of seats in the assembly, by far the most detailed of which I have knowledge, is wholly incompatible with the returns for the Transcaucasus in the Armenian newspaper, for then we would have the absurd result that the Mensheviks with 661,934 votes would have 14 seats and the Moslems with 926,905 would have 12. Actually the discrepancy widens still more when we consider that the Soviet publication allows the Mensheviks only 569,362 votes, and quite properly so, since it refuses to give them those cast for Himmet. Thus there is a second reason for rejecting the tabulation in the

Armenian newspaper, outwardly so attractive. It presents its own distribution of seats, more in harmony with its returns though still not flawless, but the AOR distribution cannot be waved aside, for it is thoroughgoing and in each of 707 cases it names the deputy, his district, and his political affiliation. If the electoral measure for the Transcaucasus were known, the correlation between votes and seats could be established. A single source (memoirs of B. Baikov in the *Arkhiv russkoi revoliutsii*, IX, 112) gives the measure as 40,000, a figure that is low and rounded off. It works perfectly in the case of the Mensheviks and the Dashnaktsutiun; then we come to the Bolsheviks and it does not work. With a backing of 86,935 they should have had two deputies, yet they got only one. That is the way it goes in the Transcaucasus—scarcely is progress registered than contradiction appears.

A third method of testing widely divergent sets of election returns is to relate them to population statistics. This method has also been tried and has resulted in nothing conclusive. Right at the outset an insuperable obstacle was encountered: no census since 1897 and estimates for 1917 or thereabouts that inspire no confidence. The latter indicate about a quarter of a million more Azerbaidzhan Tatars than Georgians in the Transcaucasus. Other sources place the number of non-Tatar Moslems at perhaps half a million. In the light of such figures, a voting differential of about 300,000 in favor of Moslems would not appear to be excessive. But the half-million figure for non-Tatar Moslems crumbles on closer examination. Of the 159,000-odd Kurds, no fewer than 57,000 followed a devil-worshiping cult and were not Moslem at all. The mountain peoples living mainly in the north of Baku province and reputed to be Moslem included one people that was Christian. A part of the Osmanli Turks sojourning across the border or forcibly annexed in 1878 would not have been citizens. And what of the 139,000 Moslem Georgians, about whom we are told nothing—would they have gone with their ethnic kinsmen or with their co-religionists? Finally, the level of political consciousness must be weighed as a factor, for it would offset to a degree that cannot be determined the numerical inferiority of the Georgians. Thus this avenue of investigation trails off into uncertainty.

The basic difficulty is that the information we have about the Transcaucasus is not enough, and that information is often contradictory. Makharadze is entirely justified in refusing to choose among figures, all of them in one way or another unsatisfactory. But he was concerned with one area in isolation, whereas here the entire country is the field of endeavor and the absence of the largest district would leave a hole in work that otherwise rests on many valid findings. It is possible to offer information that does not give the whole story yet does not distort unduly what it would have been. Let us adopt the report in the archival publication of 1930 as the framework and fit into it the most plausible information derived from elsewhere where it is silent. The 1930 report can be adopted not so much because it is archival as because its figures are lowest and hence least subject to exaggeration. The principle is better too little than too much. This source gives figures for only four of the fifteen lists; the rest are relegated to the residue, in all probability to conceal the strength of the big Tatar and Armenian parties (the Georgian party is buried in a footnote). To get the strength of these two parties it is necessary to resort to Voitinsky's tabulation, though it rests on a base more than 100,000 votes higher than the one I have adopted. The decision to lift his figures and put them into our framework will be denounced as arbitrary and unsatisfactory. Of course it is unsatisfactory. In the matter of the Transcaucasus, however, the question is not what is satisfactory but what is less unsatisfactory. And to have no vote for Müsavat or Dashnaktsutiun would be the least satisfactory of all possible courses. The total of 419,887 Voitinsky assigns to Dashnaktsutiun may be checked against the report in the Petersburg press, particularly the *Delo Naroda*, central organ of the PSR, traditionally in close communion with the Armenian nationalists, to the effect that Dashnak-

tsutiun would have "more than 350,000 in all," 270,000 in
Erevan province alone (issue of 9 December 1917). No incom-
patibility here. Unfortunately there is nothing of this kind for
Müsavat, truly the "dark province" of the election, but Voitinsky's figure of 405,917 seems reasonable; if anything, it is too
low. As for the other contestants, little is available except partial
returns from the single province of Baku, which will have to be
set in parentheses as fragmentary and will amount to little save
for Ittihad, the Moslem reactionary organization, which seems to
have had its main strength here. And so we take leave of this ill-
fated endeavor that has yielded only makeshift figures for tabulation along with the feeling that it will be pleasant to go
elsewhere.

Without discussing other electoral districts only slightly less
troublesome than the Transcaucasus, we would do well to examine a representative region consisting of a half-dozen or so districts, for a balanced account of such a region will bring out the
positive as well as the negative, the successes as well as the
failures of this study. Let us take the region of the middle and
lower Volga comprising the provinces (electoral districts) of
Nizhni Novgorod, Kazan, Simbirsk, Samara, Saratov, and Astrakhan. Nizhni Novgorod occasioned no great problem, being
in good shape with it came from the hands of Sviatitski in 1918.
My contribution consists in redeeming the Moslem and Old Believer lists from the dumping grounds and giving them their own
classifications (respectively in Tables 1 and 3), justifiably in view
of the 36,165 votes involved. Unfortunately, the same could not
be done for four minor lists that constitute the residue of 2,198—
not large enough to do much harm. This district, therefore, may
be said to be in good though not flawless condition.

It is otherwise with Simbirsk, one of the most intractable of all
aspects of the election. For the most part it remains as Sviatitski
left it in 1918, despite a subsequent study based on the provincial
archives, which evidently are themselves the root of the evil.
Spirin was unable to make any advance whatever. I have been

able to make only a few improvements, having found the total vote and the number of qualified voters, which make it possible to determine the degree of participation cited earlier. I have also succeeded in raising the Bolshevik vote to 93,000—despite the three zeros, a much better figure than the 70,335 given by Sviatitski and taken over by Spirin. As for the rest, the situation remains as it was—basically unsatisfactory. Astrakhan province compares favorably with Simbirsk: Sviatitski, upon whom entire reliance must be placed, says that his figures reflect a count that was all but complete. Still, it is sad to report that no progress whatever in respect to this province has been made since his time. We may note, however, the contradiction between his recording of a vote for the People's Socialists and then his denial that they had a list, after which he returns once more to the insignificance of their showing (*Itogi vyborov*, pp. 21, 62–63).

All three of these electoral districts on the Volga have caused trouble, minor in the case of Nizhni Novgorod and Astrakhan, major in the case of Simbirsk, but they are not so representative as the other districts in the region, since these are more populous, of greater economic importance, and more interesting as a result of the presence of substantial non-Russian elements. The great provinces of Kazan, Samara, and Saratov have also been a source of trouble, yet in their case the outcome has been ever so different through the discovery of returns that are all one could wish for—complete, accurate, and detailed. It long was not so. For many years the only source for Kazan was the report in the *Russkiia Vedomosti*, for the most part in round numbers and with the Bolshevik line missing, though otherwise close to the truth. The definitive returns were waiting to be found in a published source; L. M. Spirin did not find them, nor did the archives help him. Similarly as to Saratov: Sviatitski's figures long held sway, representing hardly more than a third of the whole until the first version of this study supplied a larger vote but only for the two main parties. Spirin's discovery of the final returns was good for only five lists, the other seven being lumped together in his catchall column. My quest for a full accounting of what happened at the polls began in the fall of 1934 and ended in triumph forty-six years later, both for Saratov and for Kazan.

Samara posed an entirely different problem: instead of not having enough, the usual problem, it was for once a case of having too much. A tabulation of the vote appeared in due course after the polls had closed. It looked quite good, especially in the situation created by the nonachievement of the Provisional Government and the Bolsheviks' assumption of power; Sviatitski accepted it in 1918 and so did I in 1950; it had been enshrined in *Pravda* and so was accepted also by Spirin. The trouble is that the parts did not add up to the whole (checking the figures is always advisable when dealing with Russian statistics). And so when a careful and exhaustive study appeared for Samara province on the fortieth anniversary of the revolution, based on the provincial archives, and when the returns by uezds added up to those announced for the province as a whole, I substituted them for the earlier ones. Differences were not great, but they were enough to necessitate a change, the most substantial being a gain of 12,583 for the SRs and a loss of 15,599 for the Bolsheviks.

We have now examined the most discouraging electoral district of all and then an entire region of six districts in an effort to illustrate the care taken in putting together the tables that follow and the successes and failures that were encountered. In line with a Russian saying, if this region were a keg of honey, Kazan, Samara, and Saratov would be the pure honey, Nizhni Novgorod and Astrakhan would have some of the comb still in it, and Simbirsk would be the blob of tar that makes the rest seem sweeter. How representative of the other regions is the Volga (the upper basin excluded)? Probably less representative in respect to having three unblemished districts, and these the big ones, causing the shadows to recede, but more representative in respect to the substantial admixture of non-Russian ethnic elements. On balance, representative enough.

CHAPTER XII

LESSONS OF THE ELECTION

THIS ABORTIVE ELECTION, so sterile in the political sense, can offer much to those who are willing to learn. The correlation between the election and the civil war has been brought out by Lenin himself. This study has mentioned several of the other lessons to be drawn from its figures: that Bolshevism was strong, but not strong enough to govern by other than dictatorial means; that the hold of throne and altar on the population had been so weakened by socioeconomic conditions, by three revolutions, and most of all by war that one can wonder whether it ever amounted to much; that Russification had deeply irritated the more virile of the subject nationalities; that the Socialist Revolutionary movement, ostensibly the "sovereign of the people's thoughts," had been split wide open by war and the rising tide of nationalism and rendered incapable of defending the peasant class that was its reason for being; that the middle class was drowned in a sea of raw, befuddled, but churned-up peasants; that Menshevism with all of its pretensions had become a burned-out force; that some peasants were already growing restive under socialist or, better, collectivist tutelage. Above all, the election foretold the trouble that Bolshevism, with its dedication to industrialism at any cost and the hatred of the peasantry that is its inner essence, was going to have in this country, especially before but even after it had ceased to be a peasant country, as has been so graphically revealed to open-minded scholars in recent years—and so assiduously dissembled by apologists in Western countries. Only this disclosure of the underlying verities of Russian society can compensate for the long and arduous road that has been traversed in order to assemble the facts of an event unique in Russian history.

Even now, it may be objected, the facts are not fully assembled. Can they ever be, and the results of the election be made definitive? In the absolute sense, of course, the answer must be no, since in some places the election never took place. It was not held in the Kuban–Black Sea area or on the Syr-Darya (chief city, Tashkent), both major districts. About two districts nothing is known, not even whether preparations had been under way to hold an election: they were the Caspian and Amu Darya, thinly populated and of little consequence. In three other districts (Transcaspian, Ordyn, Samarkand) a campaign was mounted but the results are unknown. Of these districts only Samarkand is of consequence. Thus two districts are lost to the election and five others as good as lost. Their relative importance can be seen from the seats allotted them: the Kuban was to have 16 seats (so here was a big loss, both as to size of population and as to ethnic interest), Syr Darya 9 seats, Samarkand 5 seats, Transcaspian and Ordyn 2 seats each, Amu Darya and Caspian 1 seat each. If we exclude these districts as hopeless, the question may be narrowed and resubmitted: Is it possible to have definitive returns even from the 70 districts that figure to a greater or lesser degree in our tabulations, as well as from the three others (Turgai, Fergana, and Yakutsk) where the election certainly took place and deputies were chosen, but from which for some reason the numerical results never came through?

Theoretically it is possible. The specialist can be quite specific regarding the procedure that would need to be followed. The central archives will be of little help. Not enough was received in Petersburg or Moscow because of the general disorganization and, more particularly, because of the refusal of provincial authorities to comply with Uritski's orders to send in all materials bearing on the conduct and results of the election. Furthermore, what came in may be wrong. In four notable instances I have found that what was received at the center was inferior to what remained in the provinces. Therefore, the returns for Samara and Yaroslavl provinces presented by Sviatitski and Spirin have been thrown out and replaced by figures supplied many years later by provincial studies that are fuller and that add up correctly, the parts with the whole. Much the same can be said of the Kaluga and Semirechie electoral districts. The center of gravity of any further research rests accordingly in provincial archives. When these sources prove inadequate, as some of them no doubt will—reports due from the uezd commissions, for example, will have been received from some but not from others—recourse must be had to provincial newspapers despite the inevitable loss in accuracy, the ragged, tendentious reporting that accompanies journalistic enterprise everywhere and particularly in Russia during this period, and the missing numbers that are the curse of most newspaper files.

The results of such research would be problematical, most likely a mixture of success and failure. In the back country of Dagistan, for example, voting appears to have been widespread but results were tallied in only four areas (Andii, Avar, Gunib, and Dargin); elsewhere the count was not made because the task was overtaken by the news that the Constituent Assembly had been dissolved (another casualty of the dilatoriness of the Provisional Government). Even in the case of the four areas, we have nothing beyond indirect testimony that the trend ran 2 to 1 in favor of the Moslem reactionaries over the Moslem revolutionaries. The question is whether the count is still extant and the raw materials for a count in the rest of the district have been preserved. The civil war could have taken a toll, the ravages of time still more, and the leadenness of the Soviet bureaucracy most of all.

In any event, such research would make high demands. It would be necessary to have the indulgence of the central authorities, the cooperation of those in the provinces, a large sum of money, a great deal of time, and patience beyond measure. None of these conditions prevail at the present, none are likely to prevail in the future. Whether the results would be commensurate

with the effort is an open question. The election to the Constituent Assembly has two outstanding features: a uniqueness without
parallel in the fortunes of other great peoples, and a death that
makes it all but impossible to reassemble its shattered fragments.
It seems destined to retain these features for some time to come.

PART THREE

Tables

EXPLANATORY NOTE

THE ELECTION RETURNS set forth in the tables are not perfect, but they are the least incomplete and the most accurate and detailed in existence. Every effort has been expended to make them so.

At the outset it was decided to have one general, all-inclusive table (Table 1) of not more than twelve columns, ten for the competing parties, one for the residual vote that could not further be broken down, and one for the total vote in each of the eighty electoral districts (usually provinces, always major administrative subdivisions), insofar as a total was available. In order to accomplish this purpose it was necessary to group parties of less general import in columns with broader headings because of their multiplicity in a vast and heterogeneous country now endowed with an electoral system that paid more than lip service to the rights of citizens to present their case to the public—so at variance with the practice in certain western countries, where all kinds of devices are used to choke off access to the ballot. Only four columns could be assigned to individual parties (the Socialist Revolutionary, the Bolshevik [Communist] and Menshevik wings of the Social Democratic, and the Constitutional Democratic); the others had to be composite. In Tables 2–5 these multiple-entry columns are opened up and their components set forth in their own right to give as complete an account of the election as possible.

Unfortunately, not only is a good deal missing but the accursed joint lists cross up what is at hand. In a good many instances the vote for joint lists is not of great consequence but in others it is a substantial or even the outstanding factor. Thus in the three Ukrainian districts of Kharkov, Kherson, and Poltava, among the most populous in the country, the two main parties in all three, the Ukrainian SRs and the Left SRs, offered a joint list, tying up in indissoluble union a million and a half votes and making it impossible to give a satisfactory figure for Ukrainian strength in the country as a whole. Furthermore, these joints lists were unnecessary, for a generous and flexible electoral law allowed contestants to enter separate lists and yet pool the results for representation according to some prearranged agreement. But these joint lists exist and cloud the issue; they cannot be simply brushed aside as others have tried to do.

The layout of tables follows a pattern, though it can be departed from when other considerations supervene. Horizontal progression from party to party is usually from left to right, although the first two columns, for example, are assigned to parties on the basis of the votes they received, not of the degree of their political radicalism. Vertical progression from district to district is generally from north to south and from west to east, with the exception of the two metropolitan districts, which are placed at the end along with the fleets and the army fronts as constituting special categories.

A purposeful inconsistency in respect to the election returns appears in the Socialist Revolutionary and Menshevik columns. In the former only the vote cast for the official list in each district is recorded (Table 1) and that for any dissident list, whether of the left or the right, is relegated to the "Other socialist parties" column for subsequent expansion in Table 2, whereas all Menshevik votes either for the main list or for dissident lists are entered in the Menshevik column. Why this variation? There are two reasons. First, I do not know enough to determine the party standing of a Menshevik list save in some instances, whereas I can speak with certainty of affairs in the SR camp. Second and more important, the Menshevik was a historic party with a following distributed generally over Russia, yet this widespread following was everywhere modest in numbers except on the Southwestern Front, on the Chinese Eastern Railroad, and in the Transcaucasian stronghold, where it was tied in with Georgian nationalism. And so I decided not to pare down the Menshevik vote, since left all together it amounted to little.

The Socialist Revolutionary, on the other hand, was a very large (and badly disjointed) party with millions of supporters, so that the deduction of the splinter vote is of little consequence, especially in view of the fact that the main cleavage between the general line and the left wing was reflected in the official lists themselves. These were made up by the district (provincial) organizations, aside from a candidacy or so imposed by the Central Committee, in accordance with the will of the faction in control. In nine districts, some of preeminent importance (the capital, for example), the left wing was in the ascendancy, and it was here that its strength was concentrated, not in do-or-die separatist lists in districts where it never had much support or else had lost it to the Bolsheviks. The final split in the SR ranks occurred only on 7 November 1917, and the election began on 25 November, too short an interval for the lists to be broken and the issue referred to the voters. The absence of a clear-cut choice between the Left SRs and the rest of the parent party opened up for Lenin a main line of attack on the validity of the Constituent Assembly.

As for the right SRs, pro-war above all and pan-Slavist in sentiment, their dissidence was of some consequence in Simbirsk and Kharkov provinces, to a lesser extent in Kazan and the Baltic Fleet, but elsewhere they achieved little. Hence the method adopted can be restrictive yet encompass the bulk of the SR vote in a single column.

The use of parentheses requires explanation. Many figures in the tables that follow are enclosed in them, while others stand free. Parentheses indicate that the figures rest on a different base from those in the clear. Usually their presence means that what is enclosed is taken from an earlier and less complete source in default of information from the preferred source. Always it means that another source has been pressed into service to help fill out an inadequate record even though it may not be on the same level as what otherwise would have had precedence. For a source that is complete or more closely approaches completeness than others may be deficient in other respects: it may omit partially or entirely the lesser lists, it may omit even a major list, or it may otherwise jump the track; in such a case recourse is had to a compilation representing an earlier stage of counting but carrying all or part of what is missing, or to a compilation that is imperfect for some other reason yet still supplies information not found elsewhere. Parentheses show that such figures do not stand on the same level as those taken from the primary source. A concrete example is in order. The archival publication of 1930 gives returns from Orenburg province, but for three parties only: SR, SD Bolshevik, and Kadet. The other six are passed over in silence, even though two of them (Cossack and Bashkir) are major. It was a perverse performance, all too common on the Soviet scene. From other sources the six missing lists can be supplied, but their votes can be provided for only three of the five uezds and the city of Orenburg. As the political deficiency is remedied, a territorial deficiency appears. The two sets of figures, then, are incommensurate. On the Orenburg line the three figures from the archival source stand free as presumably being complete, while the six from supplementary sources are placed in parentheses as assuredly lacking Orsk and Orenburg uezds. It is a way of achieving maximum results with defective means.

In general, to reassemble the remains of a shattered election in the presence of a hostile guardian at the gate of the cemetery has been a task marked by many disappointments, some achievements, and a residual taste that is bittersweet. The tables that follow are the product of long sustained effort without sacrifice of scholarly integrity.

NOTES AND ABBREVIATIONS

a   Irreducible; includes joint lists (except those that straddle adjacent columns).

b   Substantially incomplete; more than one uezd but less than half the vote missing.

c   Irregular mode of election: votes were cast for individual candidates instead of en bloc for party lists. The vote taken is the maximum for a candidate of a given party, with two exceptions: (1) In the Olonets district, with two seats at stake and two votes for each citizen, the SRs and Mensheviks offered only one candidate each and then each group threw its support to the other's candidate, necessitating deduction of the Menshevik vote from the grand total as overlapping that of its ally. This unevenness in the voting pattern illustrates slipshod execution of what was basically a very generous and democratic electoral law. (2) For the Baltic Fleet, the average vote is taken, since the complete vote can be found only in Soviet sources and they give only a lump sum, probably to mask embarrassment over the fact that the other Bolshevik candidate, the sailor Dybenko, draw more support than Lenin.

d   The split in the Russian Social Democracy going back to 1903 had not yet occurred in this election district or was only in the process of occurring at the time votes were cast.

e   Somewhat incomplete; up to one uezd is missing.

f   Fragmentary; more than half the vote is missing, in a few cases nearly all.

g   Jewish vote in the sense of vote for specifically Jewish parties. In addition, many Jews gave their suffrage to one or another of the major parties, to the Marxist parties, the Socialist Revolutionaries, or the People's Socialists, some even to the Constitutional Democrats.

h   No district surpassed the capital in proliferation of lists. Two small groups with a total of 703 votes could not be fitted into the table. How to classify something called League for the Development of the People or something else called Women to the Rescue of the Country? A religious list identified in a newspaper as Orthodox but not so identified elsewhere has been placed in the Orthodox column. It received 3,797 votes; the official Orthodox list drew 24,139.

i   Including some Ukrainians and a few others.

?   In place of a figure: Such a list was voted on but the result is unknown. Following a figure: Some doubt exists concerning the classification.

(parentheses)   Deficient in some respect; see Explanatory Note.

AD   Armenian Dashnaktsutiun party, far and away the main political organization of the Armenian people. In essence a national socialist party. Terrorist. Aligned with the Russian SRs, not with the Marxists.

AP   Armenian People's party.

B	Jewish Bund. Because of its close affinity to the Mensheviks, the Bund is treated as one with them in case of a common list.
Ba	Bashkir, a Turkic people in the southern Ural region.
Bol	Bolsheviks.
Bu	Buriat, an Altaian people of Mongol-Manchurian division in the region of Lake Baikal.
Ch	Chuvash, a non-Moslem people of Turkic speech on the middle Volga.
Ch-I	Chechen-Ingush, kindred Caucasian peoples. Uprooted under Stalin; survivors were allowed to return under Khrushchev.
CI	Commercial-industrial interest group.
Cos	Cossacks.
Du	Dungane, an ethnic group of Chinese origin in Turkestan.
E	Estonians.
ENS	Estonian nonsocialists.
ES	Estonian Socialists.
F	Feminists.
FS	Finnish Socialists.
G	Germans.
Geo	Georgians.
Gr	Greeks.
HO	House- or homeowner interest group.
J	Jews.
JL	Joint list. The components of figures so designated are inseparable. A figure that straddles two columns consists of components in those columns. If columns are not adjacent, the figure must go under "Residue."
K	Kirgiz.
KA	Kirgiz Alash, a national revolutionary party in Turkestan.
Kadet	Constitutional Democratic party. This primary party of the Russian middle class renamed itself Narodnaia Svoboda in 1917, a designation that coexisted with but did not displace the older name.
KD	Constitutional Democratic party. See Kadet.
L	Lett (Lettish, Latvian).
La	Latgalians, a Latvian ethnic group that had undergone somewhat different historical development and came to differ somewhat from other Latvians (for example, in religion).
LO	Landowners; in strict sense, estate owners; in strictest sense, noble landowners or *pomeshchiki* (holders of *pomestiia*, originally fiefs granted for military service, later converted to private property).
LPU	Lettish Peasants' Union.
LRD	Lettish Radical Democrats.
LSR	Left SRs after they became a separate party (November 7, 1917).
LW	The left wing of the SR party was in ascendency in the province.
M	Molokane, a Russian religious sect ("milk drinkers").
Ma	Mari.
Men	Mensheviks.
MNS	Moslem national socialist organizations.
Mol	Moldavians: Rumanians under tsarist or Soviet rule, mainly in the

	former province of Bessarabia. Their separate identity is a fiction of Russian authorities concerned about irredentism.
Mor	Mordvins, a Finnish people mainly to the west of the middle and lower Volga.
N	Nationalists.
NB	National Bloc; components unknown in Smolensk. They are known in Moscow.
NP	Nonpartisans; possibly a cover for rightists in one or more instances but otherwise genuinely representative of voters who disliked political parties.
NS	Narodnye Sotsialisty (People's Socialists)—in essence tame Populists (Narodniki), in contrast to the radical Populists, or SRs. In 1917 the People's Socialists merged with the Group of Toil, or Trudoviki—mainly peasant representatives in the imperial dumas who were after land and nothing else. It was a merger of the tame.
O	Orthodox group.
OB	Old Believers (or Ritualists), adherents of a schismatic deviation from the Orthodox church.
OU	Officers' Union.
P	Polish group.
PPS	Polish Socialist party, the national socialist party of Poland.
PU	Peasant Union.
RC	Roman Catholics.
RD	Russian Democrats, Radical Democrats, Republican Democrats, or other such combination denoting bourgeois radicals.
S	Socialists.
SA	Siberian autonomists.
SD	Social Democratic party. RSDRP.
SERP	Socialist Jewish Workers' Party. It combined ideas of Zionism and Populism. Non-Marxist.
SR	Socialist Revolutionary party. PSR.
T	Tatars.
TsF	Tsentroflot, a nonpartisan sailors' organization of the Black Sea Fleet.
Ui	Uigurs, a Turkic people of Central Asia, the majority of whom were under Chinese rule.
Uk	Ukrainians.
UMC	Local Ukrainian middle-class group.
UNR	Ukrainian National Republicans.
USF	Ukrainian Socialist Federalist party—a party of no great consequence, moderate in both the nationalist and the socialist sense.
USR	Ukrainian Socialist Revolutionary party. This party, which had by far the largest following in the Ukraine, was more extreme in the nationalist than in the socialist sense.
UTL	Ukrainian Toilers' List.
w.	With.
WR	White Russians.
WRG	White Russian Gromada; a national socialist party on the order of the AD, PPS, and others. Nonterrorist.

Table 1. Condensed tabulation of vote affording general view of the election

	Socialist sector			
		Social Democrats		
	(1)	(2)	(3)	(4)
Region and district	Socialist Revolutionaries	Bolsheviks (Communists)	Mensheviks	Other socialists
Northern				
Archangel[b,c]	85,272	21,779	7,335	
Olonets[c]	127,062		126,827	
Vologda[b]	320,528	67,650[d]		11,813
Northwestern				
Petersburg (province)[e]	119,761	229,698	(3,925)	(5,970)
Pskov	295,012LW	173,631	4,870	4,059
Novgorod	220,665	203,658	9,336	12,297
Baltic				
Estonia	3,200	119,863		
Livonia[e]		97,781	7,046	
Western–White Russian				
Vitebsk	150,279	287,101	12,471B	3,599
Minsk[e]	181,673	579,087	16,277B	
Mogilev[f]	50,684	28,446	(10,549)B	
Smolensk	250,134	361,062	7,901	2,210
Central Industrial				
Moscow (province)[e]	159,630	351,853	27,108	(6,058)
Tver[e]	186,030	362,687	22,552	(3,313)
Yaroslavl	197,465	176,035	16,809	5,637
Kostroma	249,838	226,905	19,488	
Vladimir	197,311	337,941	13,074	8,390
Kaluga	127,313LW	225,378	6,996	601
Tula[b]	216,267	219,337	10,155	3,126
Riazan[e]	397,229	251,815	4,389	5,216
Central Black Earth				
Orel	511,049	241,786	(16,301)	(1,384)
Kursk	868,743	119,127	6,037	8,594
Voronezh	875,300	151,517	8,658	6,116
Tambov	835,556	240,652	22,425	7,408
Penza	517,226	54,731	4,726B	4,336
Volga				
Nizhni Novgorod	314,004	133,950	7,634	2,666
Simbirsk	(363,847)	93,000	(3,681)	(29,446)
Kazan	264,158LW	51,936	4,906	12,813
Samara	702,924	179,533	5,102	5,301
Saratov	612,094	261,308	15,152	10,243
Astrakhan[e]	100,482	36,023	2,256	906
Kama-Ural				
Viatka[b]	(300,503)	222,272	18,964	(942)
Perm[e]	665,118	268,292	28,002	29,112
Ufa	322,166LW	48,151	2,614	16,370
Orenburg	110,172	163,425	(7,544)	(12,977)
Ukraine				
Kiev	19,220	60,693	11,613	928
Volynia[e]	27,575	35,612	16,947B	
Podolia[b]	10,170	27,540	4,028	852
Chernigov	105,565	271,174	10,813	JL
Poltava	198,437LW	64,460	5,993B	4,391
Kharkov	JL LW	114,743	18,216	57,004
Ekaterinoslav	231,717	213,163	26,909	16,859
Kherson[b]	JL LW	81,826	14,369B	5,626

	Nonsocialist sector			Nationalities sector				
(5) KD/ Narodnaia Svoboda	(6) Special-interest groups	(7) Religious and/or rightist groups	(8) Ukrainian groups	(9) Turko-Tatar groups	(10) Other nationality groups	(11) Residue	(12) District totals
12,086	1,160						127,632
(20,278)	(2,813)						150,153
22,912							422,903
64,859		(2,140)	JL		(19,374)	(546)	446,273
25,961	7,912				3,859		515,304
31,484	8,982						486,422
					176,781		299,844
					31,253		136,080
8,132	10,504	JL (2)			73,335	15,117JL	560,538
10,724	13,505				115,980		917,246
(14,494)	(293)				(22,494)	(924)	127,884
29,274	645	5,300			1,708		658,234
43,295	(19,653)	(15,910)					623,507
32,830	(4,489)						611,901
53,730	8,918						458,594
41,448		17,901					555,580
38,035		9,209					603,960
24,125		4,409			1,067		389,889
21,298	7,394						477,577
27,808	1,041	JL				7,732JL	695,230
(18,345)	(17,811)					8,453	815,129
47,199	8,656						1,058,356
36,488	8,027		JL		JL	11,871JL	1,097,977
47,548	13,380			6,222			1,173,191
25,407			JL 29,821 JL				636,247
34,726		64,658	(126)	19,935		2,198	579,897
(16,718)				(57,055)		67,043	630,790
31,728	2,001	12,322		478,727			858,591
44,466	3,030	19,641	4,378	147,991	89,853G		1,202,219
27,226	13,804	37,970	JL 53,445 JL		56,404		1,087,646
13,017	16,400			25,023			194,107
(22,404)	(3,424)	9,000		(37,781)	JL	(25,311)JL	640,601
111,241	15,129	83,734		77,261			1,277,889
15,825	10,436	11,178		529,691			956,431
24,757	(144,039)			(68,439)		145,512	676,865
21,667	3,624	48,758	1,161,033		172,117	3,072JL	1,502,725
JL 22,337 JL		(1,438)	569,044		113,965	17,290	804,208
7,951	284		656,116		123,319		830,260
28,864	14,061	4,858	497,106		31,116g	10,089JL	973,646
18,105	63,217		760,022		34,631g		1,149,256
58,302	20,870	10,479	JL+3,776		13,379	796,552JL	1,093,321
27,551	26,597	JL	556,012		86,173	8,068JL	1,193,049
53,770		17,255	JL+63,159		115,756	268,959JL	620,720

(continued)

Table 1. (continued)

Region and district	(1) Socialist Revolutionaries	(2) Bolsheviks (Communists)	(3) Mensheviks	(4) Other socialists
		Socialist sector		
		Social Democrats		
Southern–Black Sea				
Bessarabia[f]	85,349	25,569	(1,438)B	376
Taurida (inc. Crimea)[e]	300,100	31,612	15,176	6,916
Southeastern				
Don Cossack Region	478,901	205,497	17,504	10,767
Stavropol	291,395	17,430	1,836	670
Caucasus				
Kuban–Black Sea	No election held.			
Ter-Dagestan[f]	4,292	21,495	958	(53)
Caspian	No information.			
Transcaucasus[e]	105,265	86,935	569,362	(378)
Northern Asia or Siberia				
Tobolsk	388,328	12,061[d]		JL+3,733
Steppe[f]	4,018	11,681	JL+1,660	4,712
Tomsk	541,153	51,455	5,769	18,488
Altai	621,377	45,268	3,785	6,068
Yenisei[e]	229,732	95,307	4,531	12,398
Irkutsk[e]	113,378	31,587	5,534	JL
Transbaikal[b]	49,363	8,560	2,154	2,682
Amur-Maritime[e]	47,665	40,850	15,458	5,805
Chinese Eastern Railroad	5,081	10,612	13,139	
Yakutsk	Election held, vote unknown.			
West-Central Asia or Turkestan				
Kamchatka[c,f]	258	SD 9		
Horde (Ryn Peski area)	Only two lists, both without name; nothing else known.			
Uralsk	5,076			
Turgai	Election held, in one uezd; vote unknown.			
Transcaspian	Status of election unknown.			
Samarkand	Status of election unknown			
Amu Darya	No information.			
Syr Darya	Voting put off too long; election not held.			
Fergana[f]	Extent of voting unknown; only figures available are unsatisfactory.			
Semirechie	Col. 4	Banned	Col. 4	167,793
Metropolitan				
Petersburg (city)[h]	152,230LW	424,027	29,167	25,786
Moscow (city)	62,260	366,148	21,597	37,813
Fleet				
Baltic[c]	30,510LW	65,093		13,249
Black Sea	22,251	10,771	1,943	
Army				
Northern Front	249,832	471,828	10,420	5,868
Western Front[e]	180,582	653,430	(5,622)B	(2,840)
Southwestern Front[e]	402,930	292,626	79,630	(3,084)
Rumanian Front[e]	666,438	173,804	36,115	4,514
Caucasian Front[f]	6,537	6,211	1,113	
All districts	16,535,680	10,536,768	1,433,909	640,556

Nonsocialist sector			Nationalities sector				
(5) KD/ Narodnaia Svoboda	(6) Special- interest groups	(7) Religious and/or rightist groups	(8) Ukrainian groups	(9) Turko- Tatar groups	(10) Other nationality groups	(11) Residue	(12) District totals
16,545	74,331		4,241		35,428	10,536	253,813
38,794	7,715	885	61,541	68,581	43,412		574,732
43,345	642,423	8,183					1,406,620
10,938	3,205	3,078					328,552
(7,725)	(3,062)		(209)	Col. 11	(332)	(291)	38,417
24,551				(458,838)	(427,003)	(215,121)	1,887,453
13,793	JL			25,830		50,780JL	494,525
4,925	1,069	555		2,022		332	30,974
18,618				Rejected			635,484
12,108		17,292					713,946
12,017	2,299				8,048G		356,284
8,834	JL	(2,653)			39,248Bu	(6,925)JL	208,159
4,111	12,854	1,418			17,083Bu		98,225
17,233	79,330		3,125				209,466
6,327							35,159
	8						275
	87,535			278,014			370,625
	JL			JL+28,368		219,832JL	415,993
246,506	18,080	42,318	4,219		Col. 8		942,333
263,859	4,579	4,085	JL	JL	JL	4,422JL	764,763
	3,966						112,818
	4,769		12,895				52,629
13,687			JL 88,956 JL				840,591
16,750	(3,055)		85,062	(16,846)	(4,380)WR	7,433	976,000
13,724			168,354	(32,910)		14,165	1,007,423
21,443			186,219	23,136	3,386L	13,545	1,128,600
357			Lacking		1,999	607	16,824
2,072,258	1,420,379	456,627	4,796,637	2,384,123	1,862,883	1,932,726	44,218,555

Table 2. Other Socialist vote and Jewish vote in detail

Region and district	Other socialists (col. 4, Table 1; SD Menshevik splits from col. 3, Table 1)								Nationalities sector: Jewish vote[g] — Jewish parties (from col. 10 of Table 1)			
	SR Left (antiwar)	SR Right (pro-war)	SD Left (Internationalist)	SD Right (Defensist)	NS/Trudoviki	Cooperative movement	Plekhanov Unity (Edinstvo)	Right-wing socialist bloc	Nationalist or Zionist	Bund	Socialist Workers (SERP)	SD Workers (Poalei Zion)
Northern												
Archangel[b,c]												
Olonets[c]												
Vologda[b]												
Northwestern												
Petersburg (province)[e]					8,071		3,742					
Pskov					(5,957) 4,059	(13)						
Novgorod					10,314	1,123	860					
Baltic												
Estonia												
Livonia[e]												
Western–White Russian												
Vitebsk					3,599				24,790	w. Men	4,880	6,184
Minsk[f]									65,046	w. Men	(1,583)	(7,900)
Mogilev[f]									(14,101)	w. Men		
Smolensk					2,210							
Central Industrial												
Moscow (province)[e]			w. Bol		6,058							
Tver[e]					2,338		(975)					
Yaroslavl					5,637							
Kostroma												
Vladimir					6,908	1,482						
Kaluga					601							
Tula[b]			550	9,605	1,832	1,294						
Riazan[e]					5,216							
Central Black Earth												
Orel	JL w. USR + PPS				Col. 8	Col. 8	Col. 8					
Kursk					8,594							
Voronezh					6,116			(1,384)				
Tambov			w. Bol		4,336							
Penza										w. Men		
Volga												
Nizhni Novgorod		(29,446)			2,666	JL 7,408 JL						
Simbirsk		9,820				?						
Kazan						?						
Samara			936	4,166	4,364	JL 2,993 JL	937					
Saratov					10,243							
Astrakhan[e]					906							
Kama–Ural												
Viatka[b]	(942)	Col. 8			JL w. Mari; Col. 8	Col. 8	Col. 8					
Perm[e]					11,429	4,941						
Ufa					5,681	7,296		29,112				
Orenburg												
Ukraine												
Kiev					JL w USF		928		90,820	30,144	14,115	4,086

Region					JL w. USF					w. Men	w. SR + USR
Chernigov	42,329							28,308			2,808
Poltava	12,192	w. Bol						32,270			879
Kharkov			6,024		JL 4,391 JL	2,293		6,366	4,883 w. Men	1,482	875
Ekaterinoslav[b]				11,852	JL 9,496 JL	7,363	530	37,032		917	3,307
Kherson[b]					JL 5,626 JL			86,190	w. Men	5,831	1,687
Southern–Black Sea									w. Men		?
Bessarabia[f]		w. Bol			(376)			28,785			
Taurida (inc. Crimea)[e]			?	4,643		2,273		13,986			1,745
Southeastern											
Don Cossack Region			Col. 8		JL 5,049 JL	Col. 8	5,718				
Stavropol					JL 670 JL						
Caucasus											
Kuban–Black Sea											
Ter-Dagestan[f]											
Caspian					(53)						
Transcaucasus[e]					(378)			(4,860)			
Northern Asia or Siberia			JL w. PU								
Tobolsk	3,733	1,660	Col. 8								
Steppe[i]				15,802			4,712				
Tomsk			2,686	6,068							
Altai		w. Bol		8,730 w. SA							
Yenisei[e]	3,668										
Irkutsk[e]		w. Bol		2,682	JL w. SA						
Transbaikal[b]		w. Bol									
Amur-Maritime[e]	5,805										
Chinese Eastern Railroad											
Yakutsk											
Kamchatka[c,f]											
West-Central Asia or Turkestan											
Horde (Ryn Peski area)											
Uralsk											
Turgai											
Transcaspian											
Samarkand											
Amu Darya											
Syr Darya											
Fergana[f]											
Semirechie			Col. 8				35,305				
Metropolitan											
Petersburg (city)[h]	11,740	17,427		19,109		1,823				w. USR	
Moscow (city)	1,907	19,690		2,508		Col. 8					
Fleet											
Baltic	13,249	5,966									
Black Sea											
Army											
Northern Front		5,868	Col. 8						w. Men		
Western Front[e]	4,454	Col. 8									
Southwestern Front[e]		(3,084)				Col. 8	2,840				
Rumanian Front[e]		4,514				Col. 8	?				
Caucasian Front[f]											

General soviet list, above party: 167,793

Table 3. Special-interest vote and religious and/or rightist vote in detail

Region and district	Special-interest groups (col. 6, Table 1)					Religious and/or rightist lists (col. 7, Table 1)			
	Peasant	Cossack	Landowner	Middle class	Other	Orthodox	Old Believer	Other religious	Rightist
Northern									
Archangel[b,c]					1,160				
Olonets[c]					(2,813)				
Vologda[b]									
Northwestern									
Petersburg (province)[e]						(2,140)			
Pskov			3,209		2,337NP 2,366F				
Novgorod			7,804	1,178HO					
Baltic									
Estonia									
Livonia[e]									
Western–White Russian									
Vitebsk	10,504				10,040RD	JL w. WR	JL w. LO		
Minsk[e]			3,465						
Mogilev[f]			(293)		645				
Smolensk						5,300			
Central Industrial									
Moscow (province)[e]	(12,967)PU		(2,189) (3,677)		(4,497)NP		(7,467)		(8,443)
Tver[e]			4,497	(812)CI					
Yaroslavl				4,421					
Kostroma									
Vladimir						17,901			
Kaluga							4,409		
Tula[b]	770								
Riazan[e]			JL w. OB	6,624CI	1,041NP		JL w. LO		9,209
Central Black Earth									
Orel			(12,911)						
Kursk			8,656	(4,462)CI	(438)HO				
Voronezh	796?		7,231						

Tambov	887			12,493		
Penza						
Volga						
Nizhni Novgorod				48,428	16,230	
Simbirsk			?	12,322		
Kazan		JL 2,001 JL		13,133	6,508	
Samara	3,030	? CI		17,414	13,956	
Saratov	13,804					
Astrakhan[e]	16,400					6,600
Kama-Ural						
Viatka[b]	?	(3,424)CI	1,381RD	9,000		
Perm[e]	13,748PU			47,881		
Ufa	3,078			11,178	35,853	
Orenburg	(144,039)					
Ukraine						
Kiev	655 JL w. KD	JL 2,508 JL	203NP, 258			48,758
Volynia[e]	911			(1,438)		
Podolia[b]	61,560	335CI		284		
Chernigov	530		1,005NP	11,810	4,858	
Poltava	JL			1,657		
Kharkov	JL	6,493CI		13,847	10,479	
Ekaterinoslav[b]				26,597	JL	
Kherson[b]				13,038	JL	4,217
Southern–Black Sea						
Bessarabia[f]	69,085	5,246				
Taurida (inc. Crimea)[e]		7,715				885M
Southeastern						
Don Cossack Region	636,966	5,457			8,183	
Stavropol	3,205			3,078		
Caucasus						
Kuban–Black Sea[f]	(3,062)					
Ter Dagestan[f]						
Caspian						
Transcaucasus[e]						
Northern Asia or Siberia						
Tobolsk	JL: PU/NS			1,069		
Steppe[f]						
Tomsk						
Altai				555	17,292	
Yenisei[e]				2,299SA		

(continued)

Table 3. (continued)

	Special-interest groups (col. 6, Table 1)					Religious and/or rightist lists (col. 7, Table 1)			
Region and district	Peasant	Cossack	Landowner	Middle class	Other	Orthodox	Old Believer	Other religious	Rightist
Northern Asia or Siberia									
Irkutsk[e]					JL SA	(2,653)			
Transbaikal[b]	56,718	12,854							
Amur-Maritime[e]		22,612					1,418		
Chinese Eastern Railroad									
Yakutsk									
Kamchatka[c,f]					3NP, 5RD				
West-Central Asia or Turkestan									
Horde (Ryn Peski area)									
Uralsk	26,059	61,476							
Turgai									
Transcaspian									
Samarkand									
Amu Darya									
Syr Darya									
Fergana[f]									
Semirechie		JL w. KA							
Metropolitan									
Petersburg (city)[h]		6,712			4,942NP 5,310F 413RD	27,936		14,382RC	
Moscow (city)	2,279PU			2,300CI					4,085
Fleet									
Baltic[c]					1,948NP 2,018OU 4,769TsF				
Black Sea									
Army									
Northern Front									
Western Front[e]									
Southwestern Front[e]									
Rumanian Front[e]					(3,055)RD				
Caucasian Front[f]									

Table 4. Votes cast for Turko-Tatar lists and for groups of diverse nationalities, by election districts grouped as to region

| Region and district | Turko-Tatar lists (mainly Tatar and Moslem) (col. 9, Table 1) | | | Turkic but not Tatar groups | German (G) or Polish (P) groups | Diverse nationality groups (col. 10, Table 1) |
	Left	Right	Undivided or moderate			
Northern						
Archangel[b,c]						
Olonets[c]						
Vologda[b]						
Northwestern						
Petersburg (province)[e]	—					(10,800) FS, (8,574) E
Pskov						3,859 LRD
Novgorod						
Baltic						
Estonia						91,674 ES, 85,107 ENS
Livonia[e]						31,253 LPU
Western–White Russian						
Vitebsk					10,556 P	37,989 L + LA (3 lists) JL: WR/O
Minsk[e]					36,882 P	2,988 WRG
Mogilev[f]					(4,635) P	(1,385) WR
Smolensk						1,708 NB
Central Industrial						
Moscow (province)[e]						
Tver[e]						
Yaroslavl						
Kostroma						
Vladimir						
Kaluga						1,067 WRG
Tula[b]						
Riazan[e]						
Central Black Earth						
Orel						
Kursk						
Voronezh						JL: PPS/USR/LSR
Tambov			6,222			
Penza			29,821[i]			
Volga						
Nizhni Novgorod			19,935			
Simbirsk			(57,000)	(55) Ch		
Kazan	153,151	99,080		226,496 Ch		
Samara			126,558	9,036 Ch 12,397 Ba	89,853 G (42,148 S, 47,705 N)	
Saratov			JL w. Ukr 25,023		50,025 G	6,379 Mor
Astrakhan[e]						

(continued)

Table 4. (continued)

Region and district	Turko-Tatar lists (mainly Tatar and Moslem) (col. 9, Table 1)			Turkic but not Tatar groups	German (G) or Polish (P) groups	Diverse nationality groups (col. 10, Table 1)
	Left	Right	Undivided or moderate			
Kama-Ural						
Viatka[b]			(37,781)			JL: Ma/NS
Perm[e]		29,683	47,578			
Ufa	304,864	88,850		135,977 Ba		
Orenburg			(16,652)	(51,787) Ba		
Ukraine						
Kiev					42,943 P	
Volynia[e]					57,998 P	
Podolia[b]					46,912 P	
Chernigov						
Poltava						
Kharkov					5,221 G	
Ekaterinoslav					25,977 G	9,143 Gr
Kherson[b]					27,879 G	
Southern–Black Sea						
Bessarabia[f]					? G	6,643 Mol
Taurida (inc. Crimea)[e]			68,581		27,681 G	
Southeastern						
Don Cossack Region						
Stavropol						
Caucasus						
Kuban–Black Sea						
Ter-Dagestan[f]						(332) Ch-I + 291
Caspian						
Transcaucasus[e]	(3,119)	(49,796)	(405,922)			(419,887) AD (1,528) AP (728) Geo
Northern Asia or Siberia						
Tobolsk			25,830			
Steppe[f]	1,841			181 KA		
Tomsk			Rejected			
Altai					8,048 G	
Yenisei[e]						
Irkutsk[e]						39,248 Bu
Transbaikal[b]						17,083 Bu
Amur-Maritime[e]						
Chinese Eastern Railroad						
Yakutsk						
Kamchatka[c,f]						

(continued)

ble 4. (continued)

Region and district	Turko-Tatar lists (mainly Tatar and Moslem) (col. 9, Table 1)			Turkic but not Tatar groups	German (G) or Polish (P) groups	Diverse nationality groups (col. 10, Table 1)
	Left	Right	Undivided or moderate			
estern Central Asia or Turkestan						
Horde (Ryn Peski area)						
Uralsk				278,014 K		
Turgai						
Transcaspian						
Samarkand						
Amu Darya						
Syr Darya						
Fergana[f]						
Semirechie				JL: KA/Cos., Ui/Du		JL: Du/Ui
etropolitan						
Petersburg (city)[h]						
Moscow (city)					2,076 G	
eet						
Baltic[c]						
Black Sea						
rmy						
Northern Front	JL w. USR					
Western Front[e]	(16,846)					(4,380) WR
Southwestern Front[e]	(32,910)				? P	
Rumanian Front[e]	23,136				? P	3,386 L
						? Mol
Caucasian Front[f]						1,948 AD
						51 Geo

Table 5. Votes cast for Ukrainian parties and groups, by election districts grouped as to region

	Ukrainian bloc	Ukrainian Socialist Revolutionaries	Ukrainian Social Democrats	Ukrainian Socialist Federalist	Ukrainian nonsocialists	Other groups	Joint lists in pa Ukraini
Ukraine							
Kiev	1,161,033			JL w. NS			3,0
Volynia^e		569,044		?			
Podolia^b	652,306					3,810 UTL	
Chernigov		484,456		JL w. NS	12,650 NP		10,0
Poltava		727,247 +JL w. LSR	22,613	9,092	1,070 UNR		198,4
Kharkov		JL w. LSR			3,776 UMC		796,5
Ekaterinoslav	556,012						
Kherson^b		JL w. LSR	63,159				266,7
Northwestern							
Petersburg (city)	4,219						
Petersburg (province)^e	JL w. J						
Central							
Moscow (city)	JL w. NB						2,3
Voronezh		JL w. LSR + PPS					11,8
Penza	JL w. T						29,8
Volga							
Nizhni Novgorod	(126)						
Samara	4,378						
Saratov	JL w. T						53,4
South							
Bessarabia^f	4,241						
Taurida (inc. Crimea)^e		61,541					
Caucasus							
Ter-Dagestan^f	(209)						
Far East							
Amur-Maritime^e	3,125						
Fleet							
Black Sea		12,895					
Army							
Northern Front		JL w. MNS					88,9
Western Front	85,062						
Southwestern Front	168,354						
Rumanian Front	186,219						
Caucasian Front	?						

INFORMATION ON WHAT IS LACKING TO COMPLETE
CERTAIN DISTRICTS (IN ALPHABETICAL ORDER)

Civil Districts

Amur-Maritime For the Maritime province no statement was found; it may be complete. In the Amur region, 312 local polling places had reported but 77 had not. Did the 77 include the nearly 50 that another source mentions as having held no election at all?

Archangel Missing are four remote uezds with some 25 percent of the electorate.

Bessarabia Vote is for three of the eight uezds plus the city of Kishinev (both civilian and garrison) in a fourth. Unfortunately, the five uezds not included are the more populous ones.

Kamchatka Vote is for a single locality (Zavoiko) and it was disqualified as being held a day in advance of the official date. But I am including it, for nothing else is to be found.

Kherson Here the conduct of the election could not well have been worse, as Part Two points out. Two entire uezds are lacking. Two others have returns with no indication of the stage of completion. A fifth, Odessa, may or may not be complete. A sixth, Kherson, has returns from 195 polling stations out of 223. The four city commissions did better; Odessa seems complete, possibly the others are.

Livonia City of Riga cut out of election by German occupation. Of the rest, no returns from nine volost precincts with about 9,000 voters.

Minsk Complete except for three of twenty-five volosts in Mozyr uezd, these three volosts having 16,755 electors. The volosts in default are named.

Mogilev Everything is missing save 80 precincts in Gomel uezd and the towns of Gomel, Mogilev, and Orsha. Only Gomel town is truly complete in that all eleven lists are represented. Mogilev carries the seven main ones and Orsha six. For Gomel uezd only the SR and Bolshevik votes are given. These lists account for most of the votes, to be sure.

Moscow (province) Wanting are the minor-party vote in Serpukhov uezd, a volost in Bronnitsy uezd, and a military box in Moscow uezd. That everything else has been assembled and the result rendered satisfactory has entailed an expenditure of time and effort wholly disproportionate to the natural advantages of this most central location in Russia. Here the election was wretchedly conducted and wretchedly reported.

Perm Missing are six volosts, three in Shadrinsk uezd and three in Verkhoture. Number of electors involved unknown.

Petersburg (province) Vote for the seven lesser lists is known only in part. As no total vote could be found, it is not possible to arrive even at a lump sum for what is missing and to put it in the residue; thus it is lost to the election, which was as badly handled here as in Moscow province.

Podolia Three of twelve uezds are unreported. But since the announced total for nine uezds is about 90,000 below the actual total, some of the vote from the missing areas may be included in the returns. At any rate, private sources claimed that the vote in the lagging uezds was running about the same as in those already counted. The participation seems low for so populous a province, but in this southwestern backwater remote from the nerve centers of the country, interest may well have been less.

Riazan No returns from Egoriev uezd. The other eleven uezds and the town of Riazan came through in satisfactory fashion.

Steppe Votes are exclusively from Omsk and its environs. Everything else is missing.

Taurida (including Crimea) Complete except for four precincts of Berdiansk uezd with 3,400 electors in all, and for Vodiansk volost of Melitopol uezd, with no indication of number of precincts or of qualified voters. There were 753 precincts in the province. Vodianoe, chief settlement of the volost, was a large village with 7,200 inhabitants in 1897.

Ter-Dagestan Full tabulation only for city of Vladikavkaz. Otherwise only ragged reporting of major-party showings in several other towns, together with returns from a few garrisons in isolation from the civilian vote in towns where they were quartered. Nothing at all from the back country where the mountain peoples lived.

Tula Figures do not include Efremov uezd and one volost of Odoev uezd. Other ten uezds and Tula city are complete.

Viatka Full returns available for three parties only (Bolshevik, Menshevik, and Orthodox, the latter rounded off). The votes for the other nine entries and for these three in incomplete form are claimed by the newspaper source to represent more than half the total, but a better estimate would be half at best. In respect to political consciousness and organization, this large and populous but remote northeastern province did not measure up to its eastern and southern neighbors, Perm and Kazan.

Vologda According to Sviatitski, there is insufficient information about one uezd and small portions of two others (there were ten uezds). His figures have been used; even after the passage of the many years since 1918 it has not been possible to better them, except to correct the attribution of the SD vote to the Bolshevik faction. It was an undivided vote, for here the final split between Bolsheviks and Mensheviks did not occur until December 1917, after the voting had taken place.

Volynia This province is a veritable black hole as far as information is concerned. Again we are thrown back on Sviatitski, and this time he gives figures without any comment whatever. They are not in line with the density of population, an indication that part of the vote is missing. An examination of the battle line reveals that some territory in the west was under German or Austrian occupation and so was withdrawn from the scope of the election. Whether the debit is due to this factor or to failure to report fully from the bulk of the province where the election was held cannot be determined in the absence of more specific information.

Yenisei We know officially, from the All-Russian Commission, that when its compilation was made, some precincts were still outstanding with a vote that would not exceed 15,000. And we know from the Vladivostok newspaper that the area in default was Turukhansk uezd, in the far north, where few people lived or ever could live. The five other, more habitable uezds and the city of Krasnoyarsk seem to be complete.

Military Districts

The standard set for civil districts cannot be maintained in relation to the army fronts. The game being played by Russian agencies in the name of military "secrecy" led to the substitution of percentages for actual votes. But since almost nothing was done consistently, some figures came through anyway. If such tactics withheld much information from the enemy amid the conditions of late 1917, then the Germans must have been even more stupid than their propaganda indicated at the outset of the revolution, when they had commiserated with the Russian soldiers for being deprived of their beloved tsar by subversive scoundrels. Sviatitski's work still serves as the base for three fronts after being discarded for the Northern Front (for which we have the real returns, complete and official) and for the Caucasian Front (as pure speculation).

Western Front   Sviatitski claimed to have "rather full information."
He did not specify what might have been lacking. For lesser lists he
slighted I have supplied figures from earlier reports with a narrower
base where I could. *Russkiia Vedomosti*, for example, supplies a
figure for the Moslem socialists, with 471 stations reporting out of
602.

Southwestern Front   Sviatitski makes the same claim here and again
neglects to specify what, if anything, is lacking. The Bolshevik vote
has been lifted from *Delo Naroda* in preference to what Sviatitski
offers.

Rumanian Front   Same claim by Sviatitski, same lack of specification.
But for this front we have something else to go on: an official statement that the count had been completed except for twelve polling
stations with about 15,000 electors. Another estimate is that from
12,000 to 15,000 votes remained to be counted. Both are authoritative. The results from the Rumanian Front are therefore satisfactory, the slight deficiency arising not from faulty electoral pro-
cedures, as elsewhere, but in legitimate fashion from the movement of
troops. As for the vote itself, it was announced only in percentages
and must be computed from the total vote provided by Sviatitski—
not, however, from his percentages, to which he himself is not always
faithful, but from those in *Delo Naroda* as being more exact.

Caucasian Front   Only the returns from the garrison of Erzurum have
been found, and these without the Ukrainian vote. Everything else is
a blank. There are some statistics for garrisons farther back but they
turn out to belong to the Transcaucasian electoral district.

INDEX

Administrative system, units of, 5n
Afteniuk collective, 107
All-Russian Commission on Affairs Pertaining to the Election of the Constituent Assembly, 5, 51–52, 91, 121
Amu-Darya, 136
Amur district, 108–10
Amur-Maritime region, xi, 107–10, 161. *See also* Maritime province
Andii, 137
Archangel, 161
Archives of the October Revolution (AOR)
  apportionment of seats in Assembly, 22–23
  list of deputies elected, 129–30
  report of election results, 88–89
  report of proceedings of Constituent Assembly, 6–7
  and returns from Orenburg province, 144
  and returns from Transcaucasus, 126, 127, 131–32
  and village vote, 66
Arev (Armenian newspaper), 126–30
Arkhangelsk, 14
Armed forces. *See* Military
Armenian Dashnaktsutiun party. *See* Dashnaktsutiun
Armenian parties, 131, 145
Armenians, 22, 123, 127
Army
  Bolsheviks in, 38–39
  Menshevik vote in, 120
  SRs in, 38–39
  See also Military; Soldiers
Astrakhan, 132–34
Avar, 137

Baikov, B., 130
Bakhmut, 49
Baku, 128
Balloting, difficulties of, 4–5
Ballots. *See* Party lists

Baltic Fleet
  Bolshevik propagandists in, 42–43
  disaffection from Bolsheviks in, 102
  electoral returns from, xii, xvi, 14, 119, 145
  right SRs and, 143
  voter participation in, 98
Baltic provinces, 35–36
Bashkirs, 21–22, 121–23, 144, 146
Bessarabia, xvi, 8, 107–8, 147, 161
Black Earth provinces, 28–29, 97, 98
Black Sea Fleet, 38
Bolsheviks
  in army and navy, 38–39
  effect of revolution on, 56–57
  in election, 16, 44–46
  in Esthonia, 35
  influence on peasantry, 73–75
  in Kazan, 30
  in Kozlov *uezd*, 60–62, 65
  in Kursk, 28
  loss of election, 48–52, 54
  military support of, 42–44, 57–58, 63–64
  in Novgorod province, 26
  peasant resistance to, 63, 65, 135
  peasant support for, x, 114
  in Petrograd and Moscow, 37
  post–civil war support for, 102
  in Samara, 134
  in Saratov province, 71
  significance of vote for, xiii
  in Simbirsk, 133
  strongholds of, 40
  supplant Provisional Government, 5
  tenets of, 9
  in Tomsk, 31
  in Transcaucasus, 129, 130
  in Ukraine, xv–xvi, 33, 112
  in Vladimir, 27
  in Vladivostok, 101
  voting strength of, xv, xvi
  in White Russia, 34–35
  workers' support of, 58, 101–2